The Hunger of the Soul

The hunger of the soul is the first necessity. All else will follow.
William Law

****

InnerQuest Publishing
Third Edition 2009
Library of Congress catalog number: 81-52170
ISBN 13: 978-0-940698-00-0

****

Published by: Inner Quest Publishing
                                  10867 Fruitland Drive
                                  Studio City, CA 91604-3505
                                  Email: quest543@yahoo.com

****

Printed in the USA by: Ramakrishna Monastery
                            19961 Live Oak Canyon Road
                            P.O. Box 408
                            Trabuco Canyon, CA 92678
                            Ph: 949-326-3025

The Hunger of the Soul

Nancy Pope Mayorga

Inner Quest Publishing
Studio City, California

FOREWORD

As far as I can recall, I first met Nancy Pope Mayorga during the latter part of 1964. I had just accepted a teaching assignment in Santa Barbara and was beginning to attend lectures at the temple of the Vedanta Society of Southern California in nearby Montecito. It was after one of those lectures that someone drew me aside and said, "I think there's a person you should meet. She's a writer like yourself. I believe you will find her a remarkable person." Within a short time, we did meet; and, for the next twenty years, I was privileged to know Nancy as a dear and valued friend — and, indeed, quite a remarkable person.

Impressions that connect with the heart have a way of remaining in our memory. What remains clearly in mine is Nancy's marvelous vitality, one that unfailingly belied her years. It pervaded her thinking and writing, both of which were lucid and penetrating; it certainly energized her body, which never seemed to grow tired; and it was evident in the wonderful clarity of her voice. Even in her older years, Nancy's voice maintained a remarkably youthful and musical quality, "Do you know," she once said to me, "someone just told me on the phone that I sounded like a woman of thirty. How great!" In fact, she would often remark that, despite the fact that she had earned some fame as a short story writer and biographer (the story of her relationship with her parents, *We Three*, remained briefly on the Best Seller List in 1936), music was her first love.

"Oh, I'd sometimes get up and dance around the room when a lively piece of music would come on the radio. If Aristides was in the room, he would immediately hide behind his paper and try not to notice. He was always a bit formal." Aristides, her husband of some twenty-eight years until his death in 1964, was Nicaraguan. Nancy met him while she was a student in his Spanish class in Los Angeles. "I think we had a good marriage" she once told me, "because we enjoyed sharing ideas, and because we were always civil to one another. This is the secret of a good relationship—mutual respect."

However, as her diary reveals, the highest respect was reserved for her guru (and mine), Swami Prabhavananda. I should have never guessed just how deep that relationship was if I had not discovered this manuscript, quite by accident. During one of my weekend visits, I found myself searching for something to read from a bookshelf in Nancy's spare bedroom. And lo! there, wedged in a corner, its manila cover dusty with the accumulation of years, lay *The Hunger of the Soul*. Curiosity prevailed over my respect for privacy. As I turned its pages, I found myself deeply moved by the marvelous revelations it contained.

Could the author of this remarkable spiritual diary, who recorded living so many days in spiritual bliss, who experienced "such ecstatic joy as to be almost unbearable to my body" be the same woman now engrossed in a crossword puzzle (she was an expert) in the next room? Or one who could write that she spent "the whole night in ecstasy. I would sleep a little, a half hour or so, and wake rigid with ecstasy ... then I would drop off to sleep again, lying, as it were, in His hand. And now today I am in bliss and maybe it will go on all day ..."?

Until I read this account of her extraordinary spiritual ecstasies, I would have probably remained skeptical about the mystic Nancy revealed in her diary. Of course, I knew her to be deeply religious, but she had never spoken to me of any profound, inner experiences.

It should be mentioned that Nancy was quite reluctant to publish this intimate record of her inner life, and it is to her great credit that she eventually consented to do so. At first, she insisted that it be published anonymously, but at the urging of many others, she finally agreed to attach her name to *The Hunger of the Soul*. I am certain she never intended it to be read by eyes other than her own.

Apparently, a higher Power thought otherwise.

Cliff Johnson
Studio City, California

My grateful acknowledgments to Cliff Johnson for his stubborn determination to see this book printed, and to Katharine Whitmarsh, dear Prasanna, who made it possible.

PREFACE

I did not always believe in God. I was not even interested in believing. But I did want, with a terrible longing and restlessness, to find a meaning in life, a purpose behind it, a direction for it. I was willing to examine with unprejudiced mind, every philosophy, every religion, for small hints of truth. I spent many hours reading, questioning, wondering. And one day (October 28,1947) when my soul was open and receptive, it was suddenly charged through and through by something shocking, galvanic, almost frighteningly vibrant, was suddenly flooded, irradiated by something inexplicable and beautiful and altogether overwhelming. I had not been looking for God. But to cover the impressive magnitude of my soul's experience, I found only one word—God. It was wrung from my lips and I said it aloud, "God!"

Just before this experience, by accident, or so it seemed then, I had come upon a book by Gerald Heard, *Pain, Sex, and Time,* in which he spoke again and again about "enlarged consciousness." I didn't have the slightest idea what he meant. But he mentioned the *Yoga Aphorisms* of Patanjali as a guide to enlarged consciousness. I procured a copy and saw immediately that this was not a book just to be read, nor even studied. This turned out to be a series of practical instructions. I set about, simply and unquestioningly, to follow them.

I sat cross-legged, spine straight, eyes closed,

determined to make my mind a still lake, as he had instructed. When the mind was quite still, I concentrated my whole attention, with all the strength of my being upon an imaginary point of light at the top of my head. Patanjali says, "The Yogi's mind, thus meditating, becomes unobstructed from the atomic to the infinite." So it seemed. I was at once grabbed, swept upward, completely out of myself, farther than I could have imagined in my life, beyond space, beyond time, into an unlocated, timeless, inexpressible bliss.

Afterwards I sat, head bent, pulses throbbing, filled with astonishment at the intense exquisiteness of that moment just past. I said to myself, wonderingly, "So that's what Yoga is!" And, in fact, that is what Yoga is all about — and meditation, and contemplation, and mysticism. In a split second, no doubt about it, I had revealed to me the common denominator of all religions.

Moreover, there was no thought that I was the only one who had, or the only one who could experience this common denominator. No, with enormous excitement, I looked back over all the reading I had done. It was all at once comprehensible — Gerald Heard's *Enlarged Consciousness*, F.W.H. Myers' *Uprush of the Subliminal Self*, Bergson's *Onslaught of Creative Love*, Santa Teresa's *Ecstasy*, St. John's *Living Flame of Love*, the very Tao of Lao Tzu. I knew them all. I had tasted. All my reading took on meaning. All my life took on meaning. My sober feeling was that I was grown-up for the first time in my life.

Now I must say it does not happen that way to

everyone. Some people, perhaps most people, have to practice meditation a long time, maybe years, before receiving that first contact with the divine current. It seems that I had done my journeyman work during the years when I was restlessly longing and searching and struggling for some clue to the meaning of life. Also I have come to believe that I must have worked at it in many previous lives. Be that as it may—hard or easy, long or short, I can not see any lasting satisfaction besides divine satisfaction. Truman Capote says, "There is such a thing as life saturation, the point where everything is pure effort and total repetition." At that point a man can lapse into melancholy and despair, or he can start energetically to search for a way out.

It is strange, since I have always been a writer, that it was over a year before it occurred to me to put my mystical experiences on paper, and then at first very scantily. It was almost thirty years before I ever thought I could make them public. But increasing mystical growth pushed me, and a little line from Frank Laubach's diary convinced me. He wrote: "When one has struck some wonderful blessing that all mankind has a right to know about, no custom or false modesty should prevent him from telling it, though it may mean the unbarring of his soul to the public gaze."

For the most part, these notes were written at the time of meditation, over a period of about thirty years.

The Diary

LIVING IN THE PRESENCE

September 3, 1948

My guides have been Patanjali, Book VI of the *Bhagavad Gita*, and Dionysius the Areopagite. Quite probably with a teacher I would have avoided some bad moments of frustration and despair or at least I would have understood them, their purpose.

Ask your spiritual leaders if they have seen God. When you find one who says yes, ask him if he can show you. If he then says yes, you have found your teacher. Because a mystic has seen God, and all he wants is a chance to show you for yourself.

October 10, 1948

The sexual act is not a union of two souls. Never are two souls so far apart as when two bodies are closest. In essence it is selfish. The individual is self-centered, intent on his own pleasure and satisfaction. Those who write about it as the culmination or fulfillment of a marriage are sentimentalizing it. During the sexual act, the spiritual contact is at its weakest — rather, is not.

Sex, however, without a doubt has its spiritual purpose. It is a foretaste of spiritual ecstasy. It heralds a higher union. And there, as Gerald Heard says, lies its fearful fascination, its hold on us. It brings no lasting satisfaction, but it is as near as most people come to tasting bliss.

November 10, 1948

And what is the result of all this meditation, all this new thinking, Vedanta, mysticism, Yoga, etc? Well, for weeks on end my lowest level is contentment; my highest, beyond any words. I have days when, without exaggeration, I go around slightly inebriated with life. I have moments of being swept by a joy that brings tears to my eyes. Intellectually, I don't believe in God, yet my heart sings the word and my breath catches on it. Everything looks beautiful. All people are delightful and friendly. All work is easy. I am telling the truth.

December 15, 1948

God is light — beautiful- coming from nowhere, shining on nothing

December 25, 1948

"The hunger of the soul is the first necessity. All else will follow." — William Law.

Saints are not saints by chance, nor by choice, but by necessity — because there is a hunger in their souls which can not be satisfied by anything less than the divine.

January 31, 1949

As Eckhart says, "Every attempt to love sinks endlessly away before the overwhelming miracle of it." And, "It is all one flash, the being ready and the pouring in."

The whole secret is to make yourself ready. God does the rest.

March 3, 1949

Nobody can give you control over your own mind and emotions. Only you can do it — only if you want to, and only by practice, steady, patient practice of self-control. And self-denial of any kind, self-control in any degree brings a new experience of a new joy, private, deep, and satisfying. It is worth it, it is worth it!

May 7, 1949

I am reading enormously. I rush to the library whenever I get a hint of a new saint or a mystic I haven't read. My brothers and sisters! All my books are bristling with little notes I have made.

May 15, 1949

In his later years, Einstein, pondering upon the discovery of the expansion of the universe, made claim that although the universe is rushing away from us at tremendous speed, it will also return at great speed, contracting. I believe that if we are then conscious, we will ultimately know that point where matter melts into spirit, where science melts into religion, and religion is swallowed up in the First Cause.

September 3, 1949

Swami Prabhavananda —

"Know that God is the light within your heart and the light in the heart of everyone you see."

On reincarnation: "You Westerners have taken the

Eastern idea of reincarnation and exalted it, made it something desirable. For us it is something to be avoided, gotten rid of. Until the bundle of mind, intellect, and ego is melted into the Eternal, we will reincarnate. It is this bundle which desires to be reborn in this life."

Mind — the instrument of perception.
Intellect — the classifier.
Ego — the reactor, the emotions.

October 10, 1949
The soul stands steady in front of God, bathed in His radiance, rendered motionless with bliss.

April 16, 1951
This is an attempt to describe where I stand now on the ladder of spiritual exercises and experience. I owe the words largely to St. John of the Cross, for I have no words of my own, or almost none, to describe the inner life I am living.

Since October, 1947, I have been practicing meditation, experiencing at times such ecstatic joy as is almost unbearable to my body. (St. John speaks of dislocated bones. I shouldn't be at all surprised.) But lately, within the past two weeks, I have moved over into a tranquility that can be nothing but contemplation. I see a luminous darkness, and if I hold that sight in a spirit of resignation, expectancy but total self-surrender, intense self-surrender, then my whole being loses itself to burn in that luminous darkness with a sweetness and delight that brings me near to fainting, that afterwards brings tears to my eyes at the remembrance. St. John says the soul is being burned free of its impurities. I believe that. I can't help believing that. I have to believe it whether my reason wants to or not. It is happening to me, and it is pain and joy at the same moment. This morning a voice spoke to me, spoke real words, alive in my ears. It said, "Give me your soul entirely. Surrender it entirely. I will make it crystal-clear." And I could not then. But I will, soon.

December, 1951

From Aldous Huxley's *Time Must Have a Stop*:

" — he was alone, all alone with that which made his solitudes so pregnant with an inexpressible happiness…a core of quintessential silence, to which every noise was an irrelevance, and which persisted through any interruption."

" — as he named them to himself (Filippo de Neri, Francois de Sales) the little flame in his heart seemed to expand, as it were, and aspire, until it touched that light beyond it and within; and for a moment it was still in the timeless intensity of a yearning that was also consummation."

Note how frequently mystics use contradictions — the dark light, the vibrating stillness, the sounding silence, beyond and within, the yearning that is consummation.

It is that they touch a point where opposites meet, where the circle closes.

October 9, 1952

In all my life I have never known such a morning. When I controlled my inclination to make efforts of my own, I was invaded by God, purified, comforted, encouraged, reassured, in a way I could not have invented nor dreamed.

The miracle is this: that you not only believe in God, but you feel that He has a very personal and special interest in you and your progress.

December 2, 1952

The change of character which comes about through the struggle to practice the presence of God is both a means and a result. You are offered the bait of delight. You taste it and it is withdrawn. Then with great care you watch yourself to see what are the most propitious moments and states of mind for this delight to reappear. You try not to let yourself get excited in your daily activities, either pleasurably or unpleasurably, because then at the time of meditation, your mind will not be still enough for your spirit to feel that presence. You plan your day with careful economy so as to allow the greatest amount of free time possible for meditation. Your whole life becomes a conspiracy with yourself to escape into God. And yet when escape is not possible, you cannot afford to allow yourself the least impatience, because impatience, too, defeats your end. So you see yourself slowly becoming quiet, calm, patient and aloof, and you wonder at yourself, and you wonder with great and secret joy. Because all this seems infinitely right, exactly what you were made for. And there is contentment in your heart, so deep as to be unruffled by surface annoyances.

January 5, 1953

It comes, an overwhelming Presence
And I embrace it and enter it.

In eager surrender I enter in—
It overflows my soul
And I am lost in the midst of it.

When they ask,
What is this eager surrender?
How can you embrace and enter?
How can you be filled and lost at the same moment?

Secretly astonished, secretly rejoicing,
I answer, "How indeed, oh God?"

January 20, 1953

Imagine, for example, a crowd of people in a cellar, very busy trying to stay alive. They are scrabbling around for food and blankets for themselves and their children. Some of them are selfish and self-centered; some are helpful and generous even to the point of sharing or giving up their food and blankets. But one of them has caught a gleam of light at the top of the staircase. He has even been up to take a look. And he is convinced that there is a way out to a larger, brighter, easier world. He tries to tell. Many are too busy to listen. Some are too stubborn or too blind to believe. They will not look. Others listen and say "Yes, but not now. I have an appointment with a man who has a blanket. That is more urgent right now." And the saint, for such he is in this world, loses interest in the business of the cellar, which seems to him nonsense, spends long hours upon the staircase, knowing that one day, through grace, the door will be opened and he will go out. The rest of his hours he cannot help but spend, through compassion, among the gropers in the dark, trying to turn their faces upward. "There is a way," he says, desperately pleading. "All that you are doing here is an agony and a waste of time. There is a way out."

March 10, 1953

Can we insist that only man unites with God
When every bird that sings
Is tense with ecstasy?
When every flower throws back its petals
In slow, sweet surrender?
Where is the song to sweep man upward
On its vibrant wing?
Where is the pure and perfumed human soul
That dares to bare itself before its God?

March 23, 1953

You never know what real worship means until you have felt that upsurge of divine energy in you, or its descent upon you like a benediction, or its invasion like a flood of delight, or its sudden warm brilliance through every fiber of your being. Then you bow your head in recognition, in awe, in gratitude, and whisper, "My Lord and my God!" That is true worship. That is adoration.

March 30, 1953

You try to be ready, receptive at all times, and yet when He comes, it is so often a surprise.

April 2, 1953

From Thomas Merton's *Seeds of Contemplation*:

This then is what it means to seek God perfectly: to withdraw from illusion and pleasure, from worldly anxieties and desires, from the works that God does not want, from glory that is only human display; to keep my mind free from confusion in order that my liberty may be always at the disposal of His will; to entertain silence in my heart and listen for the voice of God; to cultivate intellectual freedom from concepts and the images of created things in order to receive the secret contact of God in faith; to love all men as myself; to rest in humility and to find peace in withdrawal from conflict and competition with other men; to turn aside from controversy and put away heavy loads, judgment and censorship and criticism and the whole burden of opinions that I have no obligation to carry, to have a will that is always ready to fold back within itself and draw all the powers of the soul down into its deepest center to rest in silent expectancy for the coming of God, poised in tranquil and effortless concentration upon the point of my dependence on Him; to gather all that I am and have and all that I can possibly suffer or do or be, and abandon them all to God in the resignation of a perfect love and blind faith and pure trust in God, to do His will.

And then to wait in peace and emptiness and oblivion of all things.

Bonum est praestolari cum silentio salutare Dei.

December 1, 1953

Sometimes I feel that if I sit down and with great painstaking care choose just the right words, I can describe what is meant by an intense inner life. This is one of those times. The whole purpose of life as I see it now is to practice the presence of God at every conscious moment. I used to think that such a state of mind, or soul, would be conferred suddenly when I succeeded in reaching samadhi or union. Now I realize that it is a habit that has to be trained into me, and that samadhi is not to be the cause of this perpetual enjoyment but the result and crowning achievement of it. By the time I have reached samadhi, I will have acquired the habit of the presence of God, and the moment of union will only set its seal upon the work accomplished. It sounds so presumptuous written in the first person that I see now why mystics always use the second or third person to describe these things.

An inner life at this stage, after six years of intense and honest struggle, is something like this — there will be three or four days, or a week, when God and rapture are immediately available. All you have to do is hold thought steady for an instant and relax any physical or mental tensions that might serve as obstructions, and the current of bliss surges through you and spreads out like a delicious fire to the very smallest capillary. Your mind, your spirit, stands spellbound with awe and gratitude. And these moments are not always calculated. They sometimes sweep upon you unexpectedly in the midst of some activity, in the oddest places, between the aisles at the market, setting the table for dinner, even at the wheel of the car. When it happens in traffic, it has the by-product of making you feel completely safe, untouchable.

But then there will come a period when, after being caught up and held by joy, you feel as though the same hand threw you down pitilessly for some ruthless, unavoidable purpose. No physical pain of being hurled to the ground can compare with the mental anguish of being deprived of a bliss that you thought was yours now to keep. No frustration can equal the frustration

of those moments set aside for contemplation, now so
empty of any results of any kind. If it is not deliberately
a part of a plan to humble you, nevertheless it serves
that purpose. You search and wonder and think what
you did wrong to turn you off the path that was so clear
and sure a few days ago. And you pray. You who have
never really prayed before, you pray with all humility.
And then wait. There's nothing else to do.

Then this strange phenomenon—sometimes you get
up from the most frustrating session of silence to find joy
welling up in you as soon as you start some activity. You
sit down for meditation—nothing. You get up to work
and there it is again, like someone playing a joke on you.

And it is all so personal. You wonder how you could
ever have been so glib about God being Unchanging Law,
etc. God is your Husband, your Lover, your Mother and
Father, and your Self. He hears you when you speak.
And He knows what He's doing to break your pride and
humble your heart. And He knows how to melt your Self
into His Being.

December 2, 1953
Cheney's comment on Lao-Tsu in *Men Who Have
Walked With God*:

"By humility is meant, not weakness and subservience
to other men, but that profound surrender to God
or natural harmony or Tao, which is the most joyful
experience of the mystic. One becomes quiet, unassertive,
inconspicuous, empty, that one may be filled with God."

OASIS…AND DESERT

January, 1954

All my life I have wrestled with a foggy but nonetheless firm conviction that truth is not necessarily pre-existent to man's knowledge of it. I groped around with words like induction and deduction and never could make people understand what I seemed to see, that not only is it possible that we make up our own truths from what we very partially observe, but that very often our so-called absolute truth, scientifically speaking, turns out to be untruth, or at best only partial truth. Now at last I discover, like a beautiful new friend, William James, who puts into words for me what I have long felt — that scientific truth is not discovered but invented. The only discovered truths are the intuitive contacts with the great spiritual current — truths which, of course, are beyond words.

February 1, 1954

Saint Augustine on the Inward Light (after reading the Platonists, before his conversion to Christianity):

And being thence admonished to return to myself, I entered even into my inward self, Thou being my Guide; and able I was for Thou wert become my Helper. And I entered and beheld with the eye of my soul (such as it was), above the eye of my soul, above my mind, the Light Unchangeable.

Not this ordinary light, which all flesh may look upon, but other, far other...above to my soul, because It made me; and I below it because I was made by it. He that knows the Truth knows what that Light is; and he that knows It knows Eternity. Love knoweth It. O Truth Who art Eternity! And Love Who art Truth! And Eternity Who art Love! Thou art my God, to Thee do I sigh night and day...Thou liftest me up that I might see...And Thou did'st beat back the weakness of my sight, streaming forth Thy beams of light upon me most strongly, and I trembled with love and awe; and I perceived myself to be far off from Thee, in a region of unlikeness, as if I heard this Thy voice from on high: 'I am the food of grown men; grow and thou shalt feed upon Me; nor shalt thou convert Me like the food of thy flesh into thee, but thou shalt be converted into Me.'

And if you ask a mystic "What is God?" He will answer: "If you have not seen God, then look and see and know for yourself. And if you have seen God, then you don't have to ask, because you know very well what He is." This is the only answer he can give, and unfortunately, it only satisfies mystics.

However, Saint Augustine has this to say:

But what do I love when I love Thee? Not beauty of bodies nor the fair harmony of time, nor the brightness of light, so gladsome to our eyes, nor sweet melodies of varied songs, nor the fragrant smell of flowers and ointments and spices, not manna and honey, not limbs acceptable to embraces of flesh. None of these I love when I love my God, and yet I love a kind of light, melody, fragrance, meat, embracement of my inner man; where there shineth unto my soul what space cannot contain, and there soundeth what time beareth not away, and there smelleth what breathing disperseth not, and there tasteth what eating diminisheth not, and there clingeth what satiety divorceth not. This is it which I love when I love my God.

And Plotinus, so pure and clear —

This Absolute is none of the things of which it is the source; Its nature is nothing that can be affirmed of it — not existence, not essence, not life — It transcends all these. But possess yourself of It by the very elimination of being, and you hold a marvel! Thrusting forward to This, attaining, and resting in Its content, seek to grasp it more and more, understanding it by that intuitive thrust alone...

February 19, 1954
To practice the presence of God, even if only at set,

limited periods during the day, has the effect of keeping the emotions sensitive and strung up. Not taut and nervous, but extremely vibrant and responsive. Every little thing that your eyes rest upon is magnificently beautiful, every word of the most utter commonplace is musical and, in itself, standing alone, resounds with its long history and tradition. So there are many times when I hate to go out among people. It is too much.

To read novels is always a mistake. The better the novel, the worse for me and my tranquility. The human passions, described in Anna Karenina, have permeated my whole emotional being and will haunt me for days, impossible to shake off. Yet it was not so when I read it the first time years ago. The same thing happens to me with every short story I write. It becomes a positive obstruction to meditation. For four or five days it clings to me like a too heavy perfume, and only little by little and too slowly it grows fainter. I wish I would sell a couple. I can not stand this intolerable compromise. I want to write another mystical novel that probably won't sell.

But one of the wonders of this life is this — that to read a few words about God is a sudden exquisite joy. It is like being very young and very much in love, rejoicing and trembling inside at the very mention of his name. I don't at all understand why simple words would start this delicious trembling. What is God? What is God?

February 20, 1954
Augustine's *Confessions*: "…although no man knoweth

the things of a man, but the spirit of a man which is in him, yet there is something of man, which neither the spirit of man which is in him, itself knoweth. But Thou, Lord, knowest all of him, Who hast made him."

All the little conceits and reservations He knows. To be completely honest with God, and empty, is a very, very difficult thing. And all the little conceits and reservations He very well knows! Oh God, empty me of all my conceits and send Your light into all the dark corners of my soul, so that I may be light through and through.

March 5, 1954

When you sit down, and the ecstasy of God sweeps through you almost beyond your capacity to bear it, how can you tell people about that in words? Who can feel it except the one who has? And who can understand it? Not even the one who has felt it. What is God? Oh my God, what is God? My God, my God, my God! All I ask is that you give me all of Yourself and the strength to bear it.

March 11, 1954

Thomas Merton—

"... And we long for the place He has destined for us and weep with desire..."

Do you think this is rhetoric? Figurative language? No, no, no! Out of the soul's extremity when it is abandoned, out of its sick loneliness, real, physical, hot, salt tears are wrung. I have felt them roll down my cheeks. I have been—just recently—on my knees before God. Begging.

But, thank heaven, it seems that these moments of deprivation are less frequent now and not so prolonged. How very strange to feel a constant unhappiness, unease, loss, and frustration, to have it follow you through the whole day, through every occupation and thought, to have it there like a weight on your chest or a lump in your throat. This is not child's play or a play on the stage or fiction. This is life. You are grown-up. And the tears you shed are adult, and you know very well why you shed them. Oh God!

March 28, 1954

Imagine, if you can, a lover who is beside you always and who, whenever your eyes turn toward him in love, responds immediately by placing his hand on you caressingly. That is God. I cannot achieve it constantly, but more and more frequently and for longer intervals. Sometimes the response is so strong, so deep, that it actually immobilizes me for an instant with bliss.

December 6, 1954

I lie in the sun in the back yard with my head pillowed on Plotinus, my feet firmly upon Gerald Heard, and St. John of the Cross on my heart. St. John on my heart. On my heart.

Starting here – until June, 1956 – desert.

December 8, 1955

"And we long for the place He has destined for us and

weep with desire..." — Merton.

June 15, 1956

The face of God is light and bliss. And there is just a veil between us.

I am in the midst of a tremendous surge of spiritual fervor, and it may be, God willing, that in this upswing I will be carried through to see His face.

For a year and a half I have been in a desert land. There is no use dwelling on it, except to say that probably the very worst that could happen to a spiritual aspirant happened to me — I lost even the desire to meditate, and I wandered through my days uninspired, purposeless, sick at heart.

June 17, 1956

Bliss again. Every morning, an hour or two hours of almost uninterrupted bliss. Love more fervent on my part — and responses to it instant and strong, sometimes frightening. And all through the day again I turn to Him and He places His hand upon me. I live again. It must go through to the finish this time. The veil must melt, the cloud open, I must see His face. Please God.

June 18, 1956

"Than this wavering there is no worse death, for one who has gained discernment, who has beheld the Eternal in spiritual concentration. By right intentness he at once gains success; be thou intent on the Self with all carefulness." — Shankara.

I used to think that my spiritual activities fed my literary activity. It is true, but I have also discovered that they are mutually nourishing. I meditate and write. I write and get keyed up to a higher point in my meditation. Sometimes I have to stop in the midst of writing to yield to the spiritual current in me that takes over for a moment and holds me motionless. What a rare and wonderful thing! How fortunate I am! Beyond any hope or expectation I ever had.

June 28, 1956

Two things that have been bothering me for the past few weeks were cleared up this morning in a moment of revelation. One preoccupation had been the reason for, and the meaning of the past year and a half of aridity. The other was my longing for some sort of purification—ritual, or process, by which I would be made to feel ready for and worthy of God. This morning I got up at five, and in two hours of almost unbroken meditation I came to realize quite simply and convincingly that my two questions had been answered in that year and a half of torture. It was quite obviously a period of intense and strenuous purification—either brought on by my earnest desire, or given to me by the grace of God, or both. And the so evident result is that now, with the utmost ease and lack of complications, I am able to open my heart and take in wave after wave of joy, light, love. I am sure now that some one of these mornings, with very little effort on my part, I shall be drawn in gently and allowed to lose myself in the vast ocean of bliss that is God.

July 15, 1956

All day! And it is so easy. I simply open my soul. Something else was cleared up for me today — in Prabhavananda's lecture — the matter of a personal God. I have never believed in a personal God and so it has been difficult, no, impossible, for me to explain those exquisite, intense moments when God seems to have singled you out for His particular and personal favor. He is your Lover; you are His beloved — you have no doubt of it. I couldn't explain it because I have always passed over the Atman, accepting it without much thought. And now today, simple and uncomplicated, the explanation, if I had only thought. Atman is Brahman, but also Brahman is Atman, and, as Atman, He is within, personal, your own, you.

November 22, 1956

Thanksgiving Day

The words of the Gita
Are gentle in my heart, —
Yet when I least expect it,
They shake me to my depths.
The words of the Gita
Can shake the very earth, —
And when I least expect it,
Quietly, they flood me with delight.

April 19, 1957

There are four steps:

First you are beloved,
Then you are lover,
Then you are lover and beloved at the same moment.
And in the Fourth, you are love.

April 19, 1957

Everyone practicing spiritual exercises and disciplines has at one time or another, so they say, experiences of psychic manifestations. Psychic on a lower plane, spiritual as he progresses upward. The few that I have had I have been reluctant to mention, to make note of. The reasons have seemed to me many and complex, but I think now that there is only one reason — that I did not entirely believe these experiences myself. Each thing that happens, however, gives weight to the others, and yesterday I had an experience which has encouraged, no, has urged me on to set down all these occurrences, so foreign to my temperament, so unexpected, so incredible to reason, and yet so absolutely and convincingly genuine.

My first taste of the divine was miracle enough for a lifetime. I was carried upward by the current of primal life and energy, swept out of my little self into an ecstasy, a triumph, an astonishment that nothing in previous experience or imagination could have prepared me for. Then, when I discovered, through Patanjali, that that thing could be invited, could be used by me to control and cut down emotions and ego, I settled down to a period of plodding and dogged determination, obeying the teachers I had at hand, mainly Shankara—his *Crest Jewel of Wisdom*. Then it was that these psychic and spiritual phenomena began to happen, and were, I can see now, in spite of my reluctance to believe, a great encouragement to me.

They say that when you set your feet on the path, everything turns to help you. One day I went into the West Hollywood library. The librarian, knowing that I was a writer, told me that the editor of Rob Wagner's *Script* often spoke to her about lack of material for the magazine. "Here," she said to me, "take these copies of *Script* and see if you can't write something for him." I took the two copies. In one of them was an article about the Vedanta Society of Southern California and Swami Prabhavananda. I never wrote anything for *Script*. Shortly after that the magazine folded. Swami Prabhavananda has undoubtedly been the greatest single influence in my life.

The next experience was a small thing, quite a usual experience of spiritual aspirants, but I didn't know it was usual until long after. It seemed to me quite wonderful. It happened about the same time as the *Script* incident, and just before I went to the Vedanta temple for the first visit. I sat down one morning with Shankara and as I did, the most delicious perfume arose, seemingly from the book, and enveloped me. I lifted the book to my

face. It smelled simply of paper and print. I smelled my
hands, my clothing. Nothing. I bent down and smelled
the upholstered arms of the chair. Nothing. Yet for
fully five minutes I was enveloped in perfume. I was
puzzled but not at all awed — until, a few days later in
the evening, I visited the temple for the first time. As I
stepped in the doorway, I was enveloped by the same
perfume — sandalwood incense — and I felt a sudden awe
fall upon me.

The third experience was a vision, an actual vision,
most strange and vivid. I have had vivid dreams in my
life and vivid imaginings. I had thought that visions were
similar. Not at all! In the first place, dreams are related to
experience. Visions can be something completely new,
unthought of, unheard of, and real even beyond waking
experience.

I was meditating, rested, alert, completely awake. I felt
mentally efficient. And before my closed eyes appeared
the strangest sight that an Occidental, housewife, mother,
newspaperwoman, could have. It was a dark-skinned,
dark-eyed boy in a white turban, an extremely beautiful
boy of about ten, who looked right at me with happy,
sparkling, humorous eyes. No doubt about it, he was
bubbling with laughter and the laughter was at my
expense, but at the same time took me in on the joke. It
was Krishna. I did not have to be told, although the only
Krishna I had heard of at that time was the charioteer of
the *Bhagavad Gita*. I sat trying to hold on to that vision, but
it faded from view, leaving me a memory of enchanting

good looks and laughing eyes that, as I say, is more vivid today than any memory of any sight I have had with my physical eyes. I learned, much, much later, that the child Krishna is worshiped by Hindu women. I don't wonder.

The experience yesterday, which finally prompted me to write, was the most unusual. I doubt if I can get the spirit of it on to paper. Let me state first that every spiritual experience I have had has been, as it was yesterday, when I was feeling fine, rested, relaxed, unworried, completely rational and always, at the moment, energetic and efficient.

I had come early to the temple as is my custom, and was the first one in the place. One of the girls was lighting the candles on the altar. She is the one I like to see best because she makes a little ceremony of it. For some of them it's just a business. I like the ceremony. She finished and went out. One of the men was putting the reading desk in place, connecting the lamp and the microphone. Suddenly he finished and went out, swiftly and silently. It seemed to me that with dramatic suddenness I was alone. And just as suddenly I was not alone. There was at once with me a presence which I can only describe as a tremendous impact of joy and pain which froze me into immobility. It was as if there was a hand over my nose and mouth. I could not breathe. It was pain and joy at the same moment, at that extreme point where they meet. I could not get my breath and I thought I was going to die. I almost hoped for it. To die in ecstasy in the temple would not be a bad death. I was unable to move a muscle.

I was suffocating. And when the lack of breath became an agony, I called to Ramakrishna — to Ramakrishna! — to let me go. And He did. It was as if the force that had held me swept back again to the altar. (I was surprised that the candles did not flicker.) I was left with my heart filled with love for Ramakrishna. It was a small miracle.

MEETING WITH THE GURU

year I was initiated

June 8, 1957

I shall try to be completely honest, objectively and subjectively.

I had left my mother still shaken and sick from a fall she had had in her bedroom. I had left my son inextricably involved with his pop singing group on the eve of his important recital. I had left my husband at the Kaiser Hospital for an operation the next day. But all this was another life which is growing less and less important to me. Once, Swami Prabhavananda told me that if I expected to reach samadhi without getting rid of my attachments, then I was like an ostrich with his head in the sand. I thought, "Well, I'll have to give up, then." (I did not realize that love for God, growing and expanding in your heart, can make human attachments less and less binding.)

He came into the temple where I was waiting and spoke to me, "Come, please." He was dressed in sports slacks and a sweater. When I saw him first nine years ago, his hair was completely black. Now it is quite gray. I was terribly nervous. I don't know why I've been afraid to see him, for two years screwing up my courage. The room was lovely, cool and clean, with two exquisite white roses in a vase on the desk. We sat down.

He smiled across the desk and said, "Well, how are you?"

I: I'm fine. How are you?

He: What can I do for you?

I: I may not be able to tell you.

He: Why not?

I: I may lack the words, or the courage, or both. But first I want to thank you for what you have done. (He smiled.) I have been coming up here for nine years and every doubt and every question has been answered here.

He: That is very gratifying.

I: But now I have a problem. (My heart was beating too hard and my face was hot.)

He: Go ahead.

I: I, er — (I really wanted to say, "Let's forget the whole thing," but I forced myself on.) I have been practicing spiritual disciplines for nine years. (He looked a little surprised.) For the first seven years it seemed to me that I was making fairly steady progress, to the point where I really felt that one of these early mornings I would be drawn into the center of Being. Do you know what happened? A year and a half of nothing — no contemplation, no meditation, no contact at all.

He: You mean that now — ?

I: No, it has come back to me, or rather, I have come back to it. But with a difference. Now I am not making any progress.

He: (slowly) In the first place, you have to realize that no person can judge his own progress. It is like a man walking up a gradual incline. He himself can not see how far up he has gone. And the downs may seem farther down to him than they would to a spectator at a distance who could see the whole hill. He himself will

not know how far he has progressed until he reach
top) reaches illumination, and can see everything) Every
time you think of God you make progress.)

I: I hope you're right.

He: (with great emphasis) I *am* right! Now let's see
what you mean by spiritual disciplines.)

I: Well, meditation every day.)

He: Where have you learned to meditate?

I: My guides have been Shankara, Vivekananda,
Brahmananda, Prabhavananda.

He: I mean — what do you meditate on?

I: Oh. Well, I have never had a Chosen Ideal. I began
by meditating on the Self-Effulgent Light)

He: Good. Where do you meditate?

I: In the center of the forehead, between the eyebrows.)

He: (disturbed) Oh, no, no. That's quite wrong. That
could cause trouble. It should be in the heart, or at the
top of the head in the brain. Where did you get that idea?

I: I think from Patanjali.

He: You mean the *Yoga Aphorisms*? No, there is nothing
like that in Patanjali. Nowhere does he say to meditate
between the eyebrows.

I: I don't remember. (By now I had forgotten myself
and my nervousness.)

He: You see, it's very difficult to learn to meditate from
books. They are so general. And you sometimes interpret
them wrong. Books are all right, but there should be a
teacher to guide, a teacher who knows the particular
temperament of the student. Now, you speak of contacts.
Tell me about them; tell me about the first time.

W o w

I: I had been reading Gerald Heard and I decided to look into the subject of Yoga. He mentioned Patanjali, so I read Patanjali and began to follow directions.

He: What translation did you read?

I: The one in Lin Yutang's *Wisdom of China and India.*

He: Go ahead.

I: I sat, cross-legged, erect. I made my mind a still lake. Then I concentrated my attention at a point between the eyebrows, and whoof! I was swept upward, completely out of myself. I was very surprised.

He: And then?

I: Patanjali says that these contacts with God should be a steady stream. I set about to make them a steady stream.

He: Mm-hm. Now, what is the purpose of all this meditation? Where do you expect it to take you? What do you want of it?

I: I want to be free! I am like that disciple whose head was being held under water. I cannot breathe any more.

He: Well, then, come to me and I'll teach you to meditate right.

(The relief and joy that flooded me at that moment are past describing. I knew I would be pleased, but I had not expected such intense feeling. It lasted, intensely, for two days, even while I sat in the hospital waiting to hear from the operating room.)

He: Make an appointment and remind me of our conversation.

I: But the time is so short. You don't have consultations in the summer, and they book you up so solid.

He: Yes, that's true. Well, tell my secretary that I want

to see you in June, to make an appointment for you.

I: Thank you very much. And in the meantime, what shall I do?

He: Read two books — *The Eternal Companion* and *How to Know God*. That is Patanjali.

I: All right. Thank you again.

Somewhere in the interview, I forget just where, I asked him if grace was ever withdrawn.

He: (smiling and again with great emphasis) No! Never!

I: But do you think that contacts with God can be withdrawn, deliberately and for a purpose?

He: Yes, definitely.

I: Swami, how do you explain that?

He: You must remember that progress in spiritual life is not a straight line. It is up and down. But each down is less than the one before. As I said before, you are not competent to judge your own progress. In the part that may seem to you the most down, you may be making the most progress.

Probably I could not have come to Swami Prabhavananda any sooner than now. If I had come earlier, I would have come with lots of little conceits and my mind not fully made up. After a year and a half of wandering in a desert land, I dumped many of my conceits and found out with all sureness what it was I wanted above all.

June 21, 1957

I waited in the temple with my words all marshalled for him. Very few of them got said. The interview was a surprise from the beginning.

He: How are you?

I: Fine, thank you. I hear you had a birthday celebration last week.

He: Oh no, it wasn't my birthday. It was for Father's Day.

I: Oh I see. Well, congratulations on being a father.

He: (laughing) Yes, I have lots of children. Well, and what can I do for you?

I: (startled to find that he remembered nothing of our former interview) You asked me to remind you that you would teach me how to get free.

He: Oh yes — how to meditate. Well, tell me how you go about it. In what part of the body do you meditate?

I: I'm not going to tell you that, because I told you last time and you were not pleased.

He: (giving me a sharp look) In the forehead.

I: Yes.

He: Well, go ahead. Tell me how you meditate.

I: (slowly, trying to get my bearings) Swami, I don't think I meditate any more. I think I contemplate.

(He: (rather sharply) What are you saying? Is there any difference?)

I: (floundering) Contemplation is a further step than meditation. It is beyond ecstasy.)   *no*

He: What do you mean by ecstasy? Describe it to me.

I: (after a pause) I can't.

He: (You say you have experienced ecstasy and you can't describe it? What do you mean by contemplation?)

I: (struggling with a bad time) (You yourself taught me the difference between meditation and contemplation in one of your lectures on the stages of spiritual unfoldment.) The first steps of meditation are to control the waves of the mind, to make them still. The later stages are to control and rise above ecstasy. Unless ecstasy is controlled, there is no contemplation.

He: That is right.

I: Well, I have learned to control ecstasy. That is where I am now. But that is not enough. I want more than that.

He: What are you trying to do?

I: (reaching deep for it) I am trying—I want—from two I am trying to make one.

He: What do you do when you contemplate?

I: I simply open my soul to God.

He: Is that all?

I: I open my soul and God fills it. But it hasn't always been this way. Before I saw you the first time, I was having great difficulties. I had been through a period of desert land and I felt I was not making progress.

He: Those things pass.

I: But you opened the floodgates for me. For two weeks I have enjoyed almost unbroken bliss. Almost more than I can stand. I can't work. I can't think. I have been drunk. Is there no control for this?

He: Why should you want to control it? Enjoy it.

I: But I have to live in this world. If I could find a nice cave — but I have to work to live.)

(He;)He will provide. Let it go. Enjoy it (He will provide.

(Silence)

I: There is another thing, too. I think I am afraid of samadhi. I don't think I can stand any more.)

He: But samadhi is infinite peace.

I: I have felt that I have been very close, yet I drew back.)

He: (shaking his head) There is nothing to be afraid of. And there is no drawing back. When you go into samadhi, you go. There is no drawing back.)

I: Do you think that I — ?

He: (making a gesture of reluctance, almost of pain) I don't know. I don't know.

(Silence)

He: You are doing all right. Keep on the way you're going.

I: Is that all you have to say to me?

He: What more?

I: I was hoping —

He: (shaking his head) After a certain point in spiritual progress, the mind has to take over. Your own mind is the best guru.

I: (dismayed) But —

He: No. What I teach here is meditation. There would be no point in your going back to the beginning with me.)

I: Have you no word of comfort for me?

He: Is samadhi easy?

An account of the interview would not be complete

without mentioning this fact—that twice while I was
there we both sat silent, looking at each other, and—
without dramatizing or exaggerating—in all my life I
have never been looked at that way. The first time I was
simply surprised, startled. The second time I let myself go
and felt actually as though something was being drawn
up from within me. I believe that was what I went for,
really, and I wish I had been prepared for it. In the fall,
if I have the courage, I'll go back and ask him to look
into my soul. I could not face him if I was not absolutely
clean and honest. It was hard enough as it was, and my
heart was completely honest.)

June 27, 1957

The life I am living is beyond the highest flights of
fancy that I might have indulged in before I was a mystic.
All day I am overtaken by sudden surges of ecstatic joy.
In between them, my heart is full of love, my throat full of
laughter. When I go to bed, I am sometimes overwhelmed
with bliss. I awake every morning in ecstasy. I sleep four
to five hours and that is enough. Yet sometimes when I
sit to meditate, a feeling sweeps over me that God will
be impossible for me to attain and I burst into tears—
actually. Then in the next moment I am comforted in the
most inexpressible way with a presence, personal, warm,
loving. I am at the stage Brother Lawrence describes
when I don't pick a straw off the floor without doing it for
God. Before I put food into my mouth, I say, "I offer this
to You. May it give me strength to serve You more fully."

wow!

And then sometimes I can't eat at all for the bliss that seizes me. I have lost eight pounds. I can't read anything that isn't about God. I can't stand to talk about anything else. It is an effort to work. I don't want to do anything but just sit and feel that current coursing through me — again and again — and sometimes continuously. Twenty-five minutes unbroken, it is said, brings samadhi. Please God.

July 5, 1957

All right — so I can't get rid of it. Then I'll serve You with it and love You with it and give You my power of attorney and it will be up to You to melt it down and transform it into Yourself.

SURRENDERING TO DIVINE WILL

July 6, 1957

One of the most exquisite of spiritual exercises is surrendering the will to God. It isn't done early in the game, nor all at once. "Is self-surrender easy?" asks Brahmananda. No, no, no! For it can be nothing less than complete self-noughting. There is no one to fool but you and God and neither one of you is fooled. But when you manage that complete surrender, for only a split second – it is a pinpoint of bliss unspeakable.

As soon as the bliss seizes you, the ego enters – to enjoy, to prolong. And as soon as the ego enters, the supreme moment is gone. The trick is to destroy, to forget, to lose the ego in that bliss.

Of course, if it were really complete surrender, it would mean the final bliss, the union, samadhi. But there is still that thing that clings, a last vestige of that thing that stands between you and God, that must be melted away. How subtle, how difficult! How deep the root is buried!

July 10, 1957

"... whether it is living or dying, it [the soul] is conformed to the will of God, saying with the sense and spirit, 'Thy will be done' it is free from the violence of inclination and desires." – St. John of the Cross.

First you determine to give the fruits of your work to God and it seems to you a great step. But after some time, you feel it is not enough. You must give the works themselves, the works, and your will to work. And you must at the last be nothing but an instrument of His will. Nothing on your own. Waiting, waiting for Him to act through you, and knowing that thus you can not make a false step. And work becomes joy, and you, yourself, tireless, "free from the violence of inclination and desires," unworried as to your own welfare, indifferent as to results.

July 11, 1957

No will but His. No will but His. Help me, God — no will but Yours.

July 12, 1957

And after all, there is no will but His. I could not take my next breath unless He allowed it. As an exercise, I have gone two days repeating "No will but His. Not my will, but His." It keeps me exquisitely attuned. Only an instrument. Filled with bliss.

July 13, 1957

Living in bliss, as I have been for over a month, I can sympathize with the Hindu poet who says, "I want to taste sugar, not be it." If samadhi puts an end to this bliss, then I can see how he would want at least to postpone it. For me, though, postponement is pain. There must be final union. I seem to be driven. I will never rest until I rest in Him. "One kiss of his lips and I am mad with desire." (Vivekananda)

July 17, 1957

What is it that stands in the way? It is my little ego, my will — there at every turn of thought, at every moment of bliss. And what to do, what to do? I'll cry to Him night and day, and with my tears try to wash out that last hard core of self-will. For my most honest moments are moments of tears wrung from deep longing.

And I don't read and I don't think and I don't write, and all conversation is a burden. And if I don't ever read or write or think again, it doesn't matter, because I was made to be one with God and that's all that matters. Why is there no one who can help me? Why are You delaying? If I cry to You, You must come. They all say so.

And they don't have to be tears that roll down your face. The most burning tears fall inside.

July 19, 1957

What I have to do is adore and adore and wait and hope that in one of these periods of adoration, He will turn, swiftly, suddenly, and gather me in and I will be one with Him. And now I know for sure, as Prabhavananda said, that when His arm is around me, there will be no drawing back.

July 22, 1957

It is a miracle of joy that through all the turmoil and detail of getting my son Lincoln ready to go to Brazil, my own goal is with me constantly — there always, tranquil and sure at the bottom of my soul, my Love. I never forget

Him for long. He never forgets me at all, but is always there, waiting. What do others know of love, who haven't known His love?

July 31, 1957

"The soul has it now in its power to abandon itself whenever it wills to this sweet sleep of love." (St. John of the Cross)

Any time, anywhere, eyes closed or open, in company or alone — this sweet love.

August 8, 1957

Everything is His; He is my Beloved. I am His too, and I love Him. I give Him my love; He gives me His. We grow, both of us. He grows in my heart, and my heart grows to contain Him. Soon the walls will have grown so thin that they will disappear altogether, melted down in Him. Then what was inside will become the same as what is outside. There will be no inside or outside, but only One. There will be no I and mine, only He and His. "I am He; there is not the least doubt of it." (Vivekananda)

August 9, 1957

I love Him — that has become quite natural now. But it is still a miracle that He loves me — that I turn to Him in love and He fills me with delight. A miracle. Almost ten years now and it is still fresh and new and alluring. It never palls. He is my sustenance.

August 22, 1957

More and more I am letting Him make decisions for me. Less and less I am concerned with results and outcomes. Even when I start dinner, or where I go to market are decided by Him. I wait. I listen. Then I act. I can hear the skeptics. I see my own raised eyebrows only a few months ago. Sometimes I smile to myself, thinking, "this time I'll look like a fool." But things turn out all right and my tranquility is deep, deep.

How to explain what I mean when I say that God makes decisions for me? It is that at present I am in an attitude of peaceful, unprejudiced receptivity, unmoved by desire or interest. But it is more than that too, because actually, when I let it, something besides myself impels me to act. It is as if I am standing on the side watching, and the outcome of my act is as of little concern to me as if it were the act of a stranger. Impossible, impossible to describe that peaceful, calm, confident feeling that Someone entirely capable has your affairs in hand.

Then this morning I made – for me – an astonishing remark. We were sitting at the breakfast table. A. was with his old complaint of why God allows suffering. This no longer bothers me. To me everything is God – good and evil, light and dark, pain and joy. There is no illusion. Everything is reality. I would not dare speak this to others but it is what I feel. "And as for suffering," I said (for he had come to his usual conclusion) "we have to do more than just accept it. We have to learn to rejoice in it." He started to laugh in surprise. "What a change!"

he said. And it's true. Even three months ago, I would not have said that. Now I say it and believe it, and more than believe it, I know it.

August 30, 1957

No will but Thine. Thine the decision, Thine the occasion, Thine the work, the outcome, and the fruits.

September 5, 1957

If you want to make a gift to God for all the joy He has given you, what can you give but love? What does He ask but love? And loving Him is again more joy.

September 10, 1957

What is ecstasy? It is a sweetness that grows into a breathless delight, a tender throbbing that beats in every nerve center, a liquid fire that spreads through you out to the smallest capillary; at the last, a tornado that sweeps through you, that grabs your body and twists it with ruthless hands of love. The saint can teach the lover how to love. The saint can be as abandoned and shameless as the lover. There is danger in it too. For ecstasy can become an end in itself, and if it does, spiritual progress stops.

September 20, 1957

An unbelievably terrible day. I awoke deprived of God, of joy, of life. I don't know why. But all day I fought a black and bottomless despair. If I ever doubted that I had a soul, I learned otherwise today. For it was not my body, my mind, my intellect, nor my emotions, but another thing, my soul, sick and dying within me. I went to the temple and sat for half an hour. I was an outsider. Afterwards I sat in my car and cried. I went to the market and walked about like a zombie. I was a zombie. Little by little it wore off, and I am left tonight facing myself. I, who was willing, eager to welcome pain as a "messenger from the Beloved," this pain I could not accept. This dying worse than death. Humility, humility! Acceptance! Pain beyond reach. Dying while yet alive. The soul proving itself by suffering. Experience beyond words. I accepted, but only because I had to.

September 26, 1957

With meticulous and loving care I am studying Narada. And that is all I do, besides nursing my sick mother. I get up in the morning with the Bhakti Sutras in my mind and I can hardly wait to get to them, and all day they overflow my soul with joy, with bliss, with nectar. I am drunk again. What did I ever do to deserve such love? Perhaps I earn it by loving.

(Recalling last Friday, the 20th — Narada says that extreme anguish is a sign of progress in bhakti.)

October 4, 1957

I had my usual feeling of panic, impulse to flee. (In the first place, I thought he might not see me. I told that to Swami's secretary, John Yale, when I made the appointment, and he said, "I've never known him to turn down anyone.") I wondered how I could ever go in there and talk about things so unreal, so ridiculously fantastic, above all, so intimate. How could I ever bring myself to say the outlandish thing I had planned to say? I had fortified myself with questions that I hoped would make him talk — if he was in a remote mood — and give me a chance to cool off. But I found him in a laughing mood, bubbling, actually, with good humor and friendliness. I was much too intense and serious. He remembered me, and our last interview, and he began:

He: (laughing) Oh, there you are! Well — and how has your meditation been going?

I: How can I answer that question? My life is a miracle of joy — and a nightmare of frustration.

He: Frustration? Why frustration?

I: Because to taste sugar is not enough.

He: (smiling broadly) So you want to be sugar? But there's no reason why you shouldn't enjoy tasting.

I: The last time I was here you told me you could do nothing to help me. That my own mind was the best guru.

He: The purified mind, yes. Isn't it true? Your purified mind is your best guide. Haven't you found that so?

I: And yet my mind keeps sending me back to you.

He: (smiling) All right. Come. I am here.

I: I have a few questions I should like to ask you.

He: Go ahead.

I: First I want to tell you that I make my living writing — short stories, fiction. But eventually I hope to write about God. When He tells me.

He: (laughing) You won't make any money.

I: (serious) I wouldn't be bothering to make money now if I didn't have a family. And for writing about God I have to get certain ideas straight in my head. Most of my knowledge comes from books, and books, as you have often said, are contradictory, sometimes confusing. Now — what is a spiritual aspirant?

He: A person seeking God.

I: Then a man who has reached samadhi you would not call a spiritual aspirant?

He: No. He has reached his goal. He has attained the end. There is nothing more to seek.

I: The first time that I sat to meditate, as a kind of intellectual experiment with Yoga, the very first time, I made contact with the divine current. It doesn't happen that way with everyone, does it?

He: No.

I: Many people have to work hard for that first contact?

He: Very hard.

I: Most people?

He: Most people.

I: For a long time?

He: It depends on the individual.

I: Is there an average?

He: No.

I: When you say that you teach meditation here, is that what you try to do, to establish that first contact?

He: That is right.

I: And after a disciple has had that first experience, then he is on his own?

He: Yes. You see, all I can do is guide. The work has to be done by the person himself. I can get him on to his feet, but then he has to walk by himself.

I: Do you ever take a disciple through to samadhi?

He: (smiling again) No, I cannot do that. That is a purely personal matter. You have to do that all by yourself. (I felt that he was referring to our last conversation.)

I: Some people see *maya* all around them. I see God. Is there any fundamental difference?

He: Who is it that sees maya? Only those who have not seen through the illusion. Maya is illusion. You have to see God behind it.

I: May I ask you a personal question?

He: If it is answerable.

I: The things you do, the things you say, are all with the consent of God?

He: When He speaks, I obey.

I: You are an instrument of His will?

He: I try to be.

(I thought this over. I would rather have had an unequivocal "Yes" to both these questions.)

I: I want to be an instrument of His will, (pause) Now I have something a little more difficult to say. I have no knowledge of religious psychology. Just a smattering of Yoga—

He: But Yoga is religious psychology.

I: Yes. Well—I wonder if you would comment on what I am going to tell you. You have been my teacher for the past nine years, my guide, my model. I have developed a tremendous love and respect for you in those nine years. In the last four months this feeling has become a compulsion. I can't stay away.

He: (explosively) Good! That's fine! Come here!

I: You mean I can see you often?

He: Well, come to the lectures, to the evening meeting.

I: That's not what I mean.

He: (smiling broadly) Make appointments then.

I: As often as I like?

He: Remember I have others to see, too.

I: I know. I don't want to make a nuisance of myself. But the fact is that when I don't have an appointment ahead, I am filled with the most terrible restlessness. At first I thought it was just imagination, fancy. But after I saw you last June, I lived for a month and a half in bliss. Not this bliss that has been growing in me through meditation. This was different. You might say I did not possess it; it possessed me.

He: (seriously) But that is very good.

I: I was not master of myself or my thoughts or my actions. Day and night, without effort or thought. It was a gift from you to me.

He: (leaning forward, and with great emphasis) It was a gift from God.

I: God and the Guru are one.

(He jumped and turned away for an instant.)

I: When may I see you again?

He: When you like.

I: Tomorrow?

He: (laughing) No. Come in two months. That will be soon enough.

Unpredictable. And I could not match his mood. I was much too serious and tense. If I see him every two months for a while, I may develop the necessary flexibility for real discussion.

October 8, 1957

And now, as an aftermath, bliss, tremendous, surging bliss. There is something, there must be something to which I have suddenly become receptive. In his talk Sunday, he said he does not have the power to transmit mysticism. My whole psycho-physical being refuted that statement, right then, at that very moment. He can do it with a look. I know.

October 16, 1957

Observing and listening to Prabhavananda for nine years have proved to me that he is completely consistent. And talking to him, face to face, he comes out to be absolutely consistent, absolutely honest, absolutely sure. In a world so inconsistent, so dishonest, so insecure — what a tremendous thing!

October 17, 1957

Last night I had a sleepless night, unusual for me. I was lying still thinking of a line from a poem by Chaitanya. I couldn't quote it, but I will now — "Oh Name, stream down in moonlight on the lotus-heart, opening its cup to knowledge of Thyself…" I decided to try to imagine a lotus cup brimming with bliss at the very center of my body. I got up, put on my robe and sat to meditate. From about quarter to three until after four I held that cup, radiant with light, vibrant with joy, where my heart is, at the center of my being. Oh name of God, I wonder where I got the strength to hold that bliss! This morning when I remember it, when I try to write it down, I am seized with ecstasy, my whole body seized and shaken with that ecstasy that once I so smugly announced I had under control.

October, 22, 1957

A Puritan background hardly prepares one for the impact of Bhakti Yoga. And greater and cleverer people than I have wrestled with the inadequate words to try to describe that impact. Nevertheless, I have felt that impact, and I have been given the gift for handling words, so I, too, must try. No doubt, spiritual progress is a matter of fluctuations, ups and downs. After last Wednesday night when, for an hour and a half or so, I held my heart motionless, brimming with bliss, there came a few days of — not discouragement — but a sort of falling back. "What am I doing wrong?" I asked myself. "Why is He delaying? Why is there no one who can help me?" Last night I was up again meditating and I felt not only bliss in my heart but a fullness of joy in my throat, in the very hollow of my throat. Let me insist — this is not figurative language. This is actual, physical experience. I was much encouraged, because it follows the pattern of the teaching. So I went to my meditation this morning eagerly. And this morning— my scalp tingles when I remember it and the whole inside of me turns over with a kind of rapturous gratitude.

This morning there was light in the center of my forehead—not a light—The Light. It was not steady or still. It was alive and it lessened and grew brighter, and when it was brighter, the bliss of it was more intense. I did not observe. I was not looking at it. I was immersed in it. I bathed in it. I found myself saying like the saints, "The Light, The Light, Oh God, The Light!" It seems it won't be too difficult to lose myself in that Light. It seems it won't be difficult at all.

October 23, 1957

When I heard a disciple of Prabhavananda say that she is afraid of him, I said mentally, "Hail, Sister." And I started once more to try to analyze my fear and awe of him, which seems strange to me who have no fear of anyone. I said to myself, "Let me think back in my life and remember the people I have been afraid of and why." I could think of only one—my freshman English professor in college. He was not a cruel man. All our work in that class was anonymous to the other members of the class. He was simply a man who told the truth. And not only that he told the truth, cleanly and emphatically, but that he saw it—saw it as we could not. When I came to class with my brash literary efforts, I suddenly felt naked and defenseless. Yet I trembled through three years with him, taking every course he taught. Why? Because the bitter truths I had to swallow there were the most nourishing food of my literary life, and I have often thanked God for giving me the intelligence to know that.

Of course, that was only in the field of writing, but, after all, at that time writing was the most important interest in my life. Now the most important interest of my life is the most important of all life. Tremendously important. Infinitely important. And anyone who can see through to the truth of this matter and can point out this truth cleanly and emphatically is bound to be an awesome person. When I go to Swami Prabhavananda with my arguments marshalled and my ideas lined up, he speaks a few quiet words and I am stripped of *all* pretension, discovered to myself, and silenced. That is why, before each appointment, I have moments of genuine panic, of wanting to flee. But I don't flee. Because if I know where I want to go — and I do — I also know that I cannot go there hiding the slightest reservation, trailing the smallest conceit. Clean, clean, I must go. And I constantly give thanks to God that there is one who can see a fault with clear eyes and make it plain to me with a few quiet words.

SOME QUESTIONS ANSWERED

November 13, 1957

The best thing is to forget samadhi and apply yourself to devotion, waiting for Him to make the decision and choose the occasion. Because, no doubt, it is a desire — sometimes an inordinate desire — and as such, a hindrance to complete concentration.

December 6, 1957

Still nervous, but not so bad. At least, I could smile and even laugh. After the usual amenities, he said:

He: Well, what is new?

I: Swami, is it possible for an ordinary person like me to attain samadhi?

He: Yes, it is possible. Have you attained samadhi?

I: (surprised into laughing) Oh, no!

He: Because the person just before you said he had.

I: Oh, poor man!

He: Yes, poor man...You see, we are all ordinary people. It is when we attain samadhi that we become no longer ordinary.

I: Let me ask you — has anyone here in your congregation succeeded?

He: No. No one has as yet succeeded.

(This was no doubt a surprise to me, but not the blow that I had thought it would be when I imagined him saying it. Because he was so serene when he said it.)

I: They say if you cry to Him, He cannot refuse you. What am I doing that is wrong?

He: What makes you think you're doing anything wrong?

I: Because I don't reach samadhi.

(We both laughed.)

I: Swami, to me God is so personal. He enters, He withdraws, He incarnates. Yet I have heard you say many times, and in a way I believe you, that God does not act. Is this one of those mystical paradoxes?

He: No, it is not a mystical paradox. God in His impersonal form does not act. In His personal form — what we see all around us — yes, He acts.

I: I don't see the difference. Everything is God.

He: You see Him acting, yes, in nature, in maya. When you rise above maya to the impersonal God, He does not act.

I: I'll have to think about that. Now, when you speak of transmitting mysticism in silence, what do you mean?

He: When Christ touched the man and said "Be thou whole," he was transmitting mysticism. He made him perfect with a touch. Sri Ramakrishna could give samadhi with a look, with just a thought.

I: Is it always samadhi?

He: Yes.

I: What is darshan?

He: Darshan is a visit, paying your respects to someone. When you come to see me, you are performing darshan.

I: I thought it was something more than that. You know, when I look at you, I see God all through you. Sometimes He even glows in you. Has anyone else told you that?

He: No. (Then, laughing at his own joke) Maybe they don't tell me what they see.I: They should…and when I have been here with you, face to face, the effect on me is tremendous. I have days and days of bliss…Is that you or me?

He: It is not I. It is you and God.

I: But I have been meditating on God for ten years and this has not happened before.

He: It is a stage in your development. It is not I. I am at best a channel, an instrument in His hands.

I: (after a pause) My background is so different from yours — I come from New England. A Puritan background does not prepare you for Bhakti Yoga — not at all!

He: (laughing) No.

I: And things have happened to me since I have been practicing Yoga, which I hardly believe, even though they happened.

He: Could you tell me about one of them?

I: Yes…It was revealed to me, not by any imagination, or intuition, or…emotional upheaval, but by an actual fact of experience…There was shown to me the Living Presence on the altar.

He: (motioning with his head) In there?

I: Yes.

He: You are indeed blest.

I: Yes. Yes I am. And I don't understand it. I don't understand it at all.

He: What is there not to understand?

I: Well — there was not the least question or doubt that it was Ramakrishna. Now, if Ramakrishna was a free soul, as, of course, he was, and more —

He: (interrupting firmly, emphatically) Ramakrishna is God.

I: (after a pause) You are God and I am God, and everyone —

He: (quickly) No, no, no! Ramakrishna is God!

(He made it more insistent by leaning forward and looking steadily into my eyes. I could not help but be impressed. More than that, I was surprised by a tremendous surge of bliss at those words. Even now, even now, as I write them!)

I: How could there be such a strong presence, such a personal presence?

He: God is personal.

I: ...so localized.

He: No, God is not localized. He is everywhere.

I: I thought it might be because so many people have worshiped here for so long.

He: No. Yes, God is present in a special sense where people worship Him. But He is not localized. He is everywhere. It is that you have become aware of Him and sensitive to Him.

I: (shaking my head) I was not giving Ramakrishna the least thought.

He: (smiling) There is a saying that you don't choose God; He chooses you.

I: You know, before that, the highest level of my

regard for Ramakrishna was a — kind of — respectful indifference. Now, He has my heart.

He: You are very fortunate.

I: Yes. May I come again?

He: Of course. Come in a — in a month.

He got up with me, and to my slight surprise, put out his hand. We shook hands warmly. I said "Thank you," and left.

December 8, 1957

Over and over again in my mind, for two days, his words, "Ramakrishna is God." And every time a great wave of bliss went through me. As long as I thought of Ramakrishna as a man of great spirituality, my experience in the temple could still be only a psychic experience, and I still had my moments of doubt. One thing, however, that cannot be contradicted or doubted or explained away is that, whereas before I was indifferent to Him, now I love Him continually with an overwhelming love. I can't see His picture or hear His name without feeling my heart turn over. And this, to me, here in Hollywood, the twentieth century. If He is God, if He is God — oh God!

December 11, 1957

Now, now I am coming to the goal toward which I have been struggling for ten years — a constant remembrance of God. Almost uninterrupted, day and night, day in and day out, that bliss courses through me. I never really believed it could be achieved, not by me anyway. But it is here, it is here, ever since God took my heart. There He lives, filling it completely. Oh how is it possible that there should be such joy? Joy that never grows less, never palls, but increases and expands. I say to myself, "Ramakrishna in my heart" and up springs that fountain of joy.

December 12, 1957

And this was none of my doing. This was all His. It's true — I did not choose Him; He chose me. And I die of joy!

December 20, 1957

Still very nervous in his presence. Perhaps there is an insincerity in me that makes me feel insecure.

He: How are you?

I: Fine, thank you. You told me to come back in a month, but this question could not wait. If you will answer it for me, I won't bother you for a long time.

He: (smiling) What is this question?

I: How do you know that Ramakrishna is God? How can you say so with such conviction?

He: Oh, I can't answer that question. That is something you have to answer for yourself.

I: If you would just say that you know —

He: But that would not convince you, to have me say it.

I: Yes it would.

He: Well, I can say it, certainly I can say it. He is God. He is the Blessed Lord Himself.

(I sat back silent, unconvinced. He was right.)

I: The trouble is I never could accept the idea of God in human form, God hanging from the cross, God dying of indigestion, God —

He: It is not God on the cross. God has put on this human form but He is not bound by it. As a matter of fact, He is in everyone, in you, in me —

I: Yes, yes, I agree with that. And in Ramakrishna and Christ He was more manifest. They were men of the highest spirituality. But you mean something more than that.

He: Yes. (Pause) It is not necessary for you to believe that Ramakrishna is God. He Himself never asked anyone to.

I: Yes, it is necessary. You know what happened to me here in the temple. As long as I think of Ramakrishna as a very spiritual man, I will have doubts.

He: (shaking his head) I cannot help you. Only you can convince yourself.

I: There is just one thing that cannot be denied, and that is that before I felt Ramakrishna on the altar, He was nothing to me. In the space of a few minutes, He became everything. I can't say that He isn't God. What shall I do?

He: Pray. Ask Him.

I: You know, I am not able to work. Once before, I told you this and you said, "He will provide." Will you say that again?

He: I can't say anything to you if you doubt.

I: Please say it.

He: Of course He will provide. He provides for you, for me, for that tree out there, for that bird in it. He provides for everyone and everything.

(I sat silent, sick at heart. I don't know why. I guess because of my own stubbornness.)

I: Do you think I am psychopathic?

He: (laughing a little) No.

I: I used to be such a cool and reasonable person. Ramakrishna has ruined my life.

(Silence)

He: What you must do is pray. Pray for knowledge, for light, for guidance. It will come.

Now, the day after, as usual, the high point of the talk stands out, and what I remember is his face—his face when he stated that Ramakrishna is God. He looked away for a minute as though I had stumbled upon some private secret of his own. And his eyes, when he spoke, were certainly remembering something great and full of wonder. I waited for him and held the door for him as we came out of the temple—a little man, growing old, but with a gigantic spirituality that can definitely be felt. I had cancelled my January appointment, because I don't want to impose on him, but already I am wondering how soon I can make another.

December 22, 1957

I have seen the Light in the center of the forehead. It is incredibly beautiful, incredibly beautiful! (Written in the midst of meditation this morning.)

The effect of an illumined teacher is subtle, incomprehensible and unfailing. To this I bear witness. He hardly ever says what I expect or want him to say. But when I get home, the words he has said grow in my heart — grow into fullness of joy, bliss, satisfaction.

December 26, 1957

Did I ever have doubts? It was my intellect. When I threw the intellect out the window, the heart took over. I have been through the fire. I don't think I'll ever doubt again.

I understand. I understand everyone and everything. I understand Ramakrishna crying and rubbing his face in the ground. I understand him in his last illness. If someone told me that meditating on God is bad for the health, could I stop? Impossible now. He owns me. The last obstacle has gone. I am ready whenever He wants me. To be an instrument of Your will, Oh God! I live in bliss.

"ONLY GOD! NOTHING BUT GOD!"

January 9, 1958

God is the Self of my self, within my heart. It is such exquisite joy to surrender to Him.

January 10, 1958

No will but Thine. No desires but the one. God, help me. It is going to take far more effort and dedication than I have put forth up to now. I will not get up from under this tree until I achieve. I will not even think of anything else.

January 14, 1958

The indisputable fact is—I even feel reluctant to write it—that I get messages. I get instructions. I used to doubt them, argue with them, deny them even. I used to try to rationalize them—to say they came from my subconscious, or that they were the result of wishful thinking. But this line of reasoning does not hold up, because, in the first place, the words spoken to me, if not against my wishes, at least disregard or do not take into account any wishes of mine. In the second place, they are spoken with an assurance and authority that I never feel in my own words. This morning: For weeks I have been feeling desperate about samadhi, wanting it with desperation. Then while I was meditating this morning I saw myself—not in a vision, just in my mind's eye—kneeling in supplication. There was nothing unusual about it. It has been my mental attitude for months. But this time there were words answering my supplication, words which said with insistence and authority, "Wait. Be patient. Enjoy the bliss of the Atman."

January 17, 1958

It was beautiful the way Swami did it—last night— "There is this infinite sea of bliss, and you are in the middle of it, just a geometrical point. And then"—he lifted his hand suddenly and swept away that little point. When he spoke, his voice was almost a whisper, "—only God! Nothing but God!"

My breath was snatched away from me. I shut my eyes. The blood rushed to my face and the stab of joy in me was as sharp as a knife.

January 20, 1958

This morning I answered the message I received a few mornings ago—"O God, Thy will be done in me perfectly—in Your own time, in Your own way."

The bliss of the Atman can be felt in an infinite number of ways—infinite variety—but the best, the sweetest, the most blissful, is the Light.

Time disappears completely, absolutely. I close my eyes to meditate. For just a couple of minutes, just a couple of minutes, I contemplate that ineffable Light, exclaiming to myself over it, asking for more—more Light, more Light! And when at last I open my eyes, reluctantly, two hours have passed, two hours by the clock. No time there. No markings, no limits — an infinite, uncharted sea of blissful light. I am on the shore of it. The aim, as Swami Prabhavananda said, is to be in the midst of it, to be just a geometrical point which at last disappears altogether, swallowed up, faded out. Only Light! Only God!

February 4, 1958

The heart of Ramakrishna has its center everywhere, its circumference nowhere. It is allpervading, and I am That.

February 14, 1958

For some time I have been thinking that I ought to mention that the notes in this book are mostly made in "up" periods. But movement in spiritual growth is by no means steadily up. There are not only slumps, but also wide plateaus — peaceful but unprogressive rest periods. There are times, too, of desperate clinging, to hold the foothold won. And then, of course, periods of depression, periods of doubt. Spiritual depression is terrible, dark and bitter. But I believe doubt is worse. Because in depression you know you'll come out of it sooner or later. You even know that the fight out of it will leave you better, higher. But when doubt comes, when you begin to wonder, "What am I doing? Is this all nonsense? Does it really lead anywhere?" — That is a very bad time. It is a bad time because you have already been convinced that the ordinary life of the world is sterile.

There is no going back. If the new life you have chosen is a delusion, then you are caught between, dancing at the end of a rope with your feet in the air. Doubt is much harder to conquer than depression. Nothing works. Conviction can come only from within, and within is hollow with doubt. But Brahmananda says: "Doubt will come until you have realized God; therefore you must hold fast to God and pray." And Prabhavananda: "What you must do is pray. Pray for knowledge, for light, for guidance. It will come."

March 6, 1958

I used to think that people who claimed they did everything for God were posing. Brother Lawrence I could not dismiss that way, but I thought he was a sort of childlike freak. Now I know it is so, it can be done, it is natural, it gets to be part of you. The cup I am drinking from — sometimes I feel I can't put it back on the saucer without His permission. Often these days I have a strong and firm feeling that He is taking care of every minute detail of my life. The less I think about my actions, the better they go.

March 9, 1958

In the practicing mystic, the average, adulterated emotions become pure, strong, and sharp. When, for example, you have made a resolution to keep the stream of your thought flowing toward God, and you allow yourself to become annoyed or to be drawn into an argument, you forget your resolution, not only for the moment, but perhaps for hours afterwards. Then you are sorry. Then you are really sorry. There is true, strong, sharp remorse as you never ever felt it in the old days. The wise man does not argue.

March 13, 1958

And gratitude! Gratitude is so full, so complete. Thank You for life and the opportunity it brings. Thank You for health and intelligence. Thank You for the whole chain of circumstances that brought me to my knees in front of You. My heart is constantly full of gratitude.

March 20, 1958

For a year I have kept a picture of Ramakrishna in a place of honor in my room, and it is interesting that a sort of companionship has grown between us. He is there when I go to bed and when I wake up in the morning and every time I step in the doorway. When I am away from my room, I think of him waiting there. More than that, sometimes I feel drawn to go, just for a minute, to greet him. This is just the picture for which I have a kind of sister-brother affection. What has happened in my heart where the spirit of Ramakrishna lives, I cannot even try to describe. He owns me. And just a thought of Him can make my heart surge toward Him in a tremendous wave of bliss. I am learning to control this wave at the center of my being, and I hope eventually to be able to channel this marvel, this prodigious energy, upward, to meet

Him there where he waits — to join Him in ultimate and infinite bliss. Ramakrishna! Ramakrishna!

March 26, 1958

The universe has a drift. I felt it this morning in meditation. It was unvarying and in one direction.

March 31, 1958

I should like to put my finger on that delicate and elusive phenomenon of conversion. What is it? The effect, of course, is psychological. But that is only one side of it. The cause? There has been something, perhaps, for a long time, pressing in upon the psyche, until at last the barrier of the psyche gives way — sometimes in a blinding flash of light, as with Paul on the Damascus road — sometimes gently, almost imperceptibly as with me. Paul was fighting the pressure. I was not even aware of it. The pressure was gradual and gentle, gentle as Ramakrishna Himself. But just the same, there came that moment of breakthrough, which took me by surprise and left me astonished by this overwhelming love for God — at every moment of the day, with every breath I take.

April 2, 1958

He was behind schedule, so I sat in the temple and prayed hard to Ramakrishna for the success of this interview. And at the time I did not know exactly what I meant by that success, but now I do. I meant that I wanted to feel and come away with a small part of the inestimable riches of his presence — of what he stands for and what he gives out. My prayer was answered in overflowing abundance. I am filled today, my heart brimming over with light and bliss.

He: Well, and how are you?

I: Fine: And you? Have you fully recovered from your flu?

He: Oh yes.

I: It's terrible without you here.

He: (smiling broadly) But God is everywhere. Never absent.

I: Well, but a piece of God is missing.

He: (laughing) Oh no! A piece of God! Well, and how have things been going?

I: I have something I want to tell you. It may not interest you, but if you will listen, it will give me such joy to tell you. First, though, there are a couple of things I want to get straightened out. I read in so many of the Scriptures that the bhakta wants only to love and serve. He doesn't ask for freedom. Now, I think of myself as a bhakta, but sometimes I am — desperate for samadhi — most of the time. Is that a mistake?

He: Samadhi does not mean freedom, you know. Freedom is not-being-reborn.

I: But samadhi does bring freedom?

He: Oh yes. Your karmas are wiped out. But you may choose to be reborn. For the good of mankind.

I: A Bodhisattva.

He: Yes. But you should desire samadhi. You should pray for it, cry for it, be desperate for it.

I: Then it's not selfish to desire freedom for yourself?

He: No, it is not selfish. The desire for freedom is not a selfish desire.

I: I wish I had come to you sooner. I got some very strange ideas on my own. Swami, the first time I meditated, I succeeded. And I thought that was the way it happened to everyone. Then when I began to see God in you — actually, not figuratively — I thought of course many people would have seen that and mentioned it to you. I was quite surprised. Now let me ask you this — last spring Sri Ramakrishna revealed His Presence to me here in the temple. Have many others had that experience?

He: Well, that's what everyone is striving for. That's what they come here for.

I: But this happened. It was an experience, a fact.

He: (shaking his head) You musn't get the idea that your experience is unique. It is not.

I: I have the feeling that He wants something of me.

He: (shaking his head) If He wants something of you, you will know it at the right time.

I: I suppose so. You know, I never practiced ritual. I never prayed to Ramakrishna. I didn't believe in His Divinity. I even had great doubts about the validity of that experience. When I came to you with my doubts, you said, each time, "Ramakrishna — is — God." Even then — it took a little time — but what I came to tell you today is that now I know. He is the Blessed Lord Himself. There is no doubt.

He: (very intensely) No, there is no doubt. Ramakrishna is God. There is no doubt about it.

I: But now, you see, something else has happened. Since Ramakrishna took my heart, everything else has been tedious and boring and stupid!

He: (laughing with genuine relish) Yes, yes! That happens, too.

I: The worst of it is that my work suffers. Swami, I have been a writer for 25 years, but since last April — April 28 — I haven't written anything that I could send to my agent. And I have been wondering — if I were your disciple and you had my spiritual welfare at heart, would you consider — would you say that I was justified in giving up work, giving up trying to work, and devoting all my time to God?

(Before I had finished, he was shaking his head emphatically.)

He: No. No. You must work. It is very important. Work and worship should go hand in hand, harmoniously.

I: That's the trouble. In my life it's a tug-of-war.

He: No, no. You must work. You must make yourself work. Pray to Ramakrishna. He will help you. Dedicate your work to Him. Work should be offered as a worship. That's the way to do it.

I: You have said that thousands of times.

He: (smiling) Yes.

I: — and I have heard you say it hundreds of times. But would you tell me once more how to work?

He: Yes. I will. (He leaned forward, clasping his hands on the desk, and looked with great compassion into my eyes.) You are a writer. Before you sit down to write, pray

to Ramakrishna. Tell Him the work is for Him. Ask Him
to give you inspiration. Ask Him to do it. He will. Then,
of course, when you have finished working, thank Him
for His help, and offer the work you have done to Him.
This way you will work better, and it will be better work.

I: Will it?

He: Yes, it will.

I: I'll try — I'll try — and thank you. May I come again?

He: (with great cordiality) Surely. Of course. Come!

His eyes are so intense that they have a tremendous
effect on me always. The simple things he said about
working were living, burning words because of the
intensity with which he looked into my face as he leaned
across the desk toward me. He meant and felt every word
that he spoke, and I felt them deep in me, touching my
heart. They were unbelievably soothing to the trouble
that had been hurting inside of me for weeks. I started to
go home, then changed my mind and went back to sit in
the temple. I was alone, and I wept. I don't know why.

I love him so. But not for himself, but for that which
is inside of him, which I have seen with my eyes,
glowing in him — that for which my soul hungers and
thirsts and which comes from him so easily, so freely,
so generously — from his voice, from his eyes, from that
almost tangible aura of spirituality, which I can feel
so strongly when I am near him. I held the door of the
temple for him as we left together. It gives me exquisite
pleasure to hold the door for him. He acknowledges it
gravely without a word.

April 4, 1958

One of the terrifying, yet ultimately satisfying, things that Swami Prabhavananda does in his interviews, is to strip off pretension. I remember reading an article of mine that Reader's Digest had picked up, and being greatly embarrassed to find that they had said everything that I had said in a third of the words.

When I am going to consult Prabhavananda, I always write what I intend to say — every word — and then I memorize the main points and questions. This is because he can, and often does, throw my mind into a disorganized whirl with one or two pointed, perceptive words. But when I start to say my carefully composed piece, and he is looking at me intently, I find myself leaving out adjectives, toning down superlatives. I am always forced, finally, to face the essential reason why I came, and sometimes I have not stated that reason even to myself. Sometimes it comes stammering out in fright. Then, it is honest. Little by little, all that is false is being pared away. Little by little I feel him drawing me up. Sometimes it has been extremely painful. Nothing hurts more than the withering of the beautiful flower of ego under the steady, inescapable look of spiritual discernment in his eyes.

And he is so wise to catch the first, almost imperceptible budding of new self-satisfaction. Witness the last interview. How quickly, how firmly he shook his head at the very first hint I gave of considering myself unique. Good. Good. It was building in me, I know. I feel clean and strong now. The sea of light is established in my forehead, and it washed over me this morning in wave after wave of purifying bliss. To break away, to think of work is monstrously difficult.

April 11, 1958

Last night he said, "We intellectuals find it difficult to accept a personal God, a divine incarnation." Then he dropped his voice, as he often does for emphasis, to a tone confidential and full of wonder. "But, you know, He takes our hearts. We don't know how." My emotions, which have been so tender on that subject lately, were taken by surprise, and I had to close my eyes to keep back the tears.

This started me again thinking of conversion. It seems to me there is a pressure on the psyche and that pressure is Love, God's Love. After a while, the barrier of the psyche gives way. Love rushes in, and with it conviction. No more doubt. Conversion.

April 30, 1958

There comes a moment when your whole being goes forth to Him in one great wordless surge of love and longing. That is prayer.

May 2, 1958

My question at the class last night was: Why do some free souls choose to be Bodhisattvas, and why don't all free souls choose to be? His answer, substantially, was this: "I think it is a matter of capacity. Some souls have a greater capacity for spirituality. You can't put two quarts of liquid into a one-quart vessel. Some smaller souls cannot hold the power that enters them and cannot control it. It sweeps them upward. They go straight to God. But great souls, strong souls, like Vivekananda, can control that spirituality, channel it and use it for the good of mankind. But they are born to it. I don't believe they choose."

May 20, 1958

I am reminded of St. Francis of Sales — "For God's sake keep healthy." A migraine, the effects of which lasted about a week, set me back. Just now my mornings are beginning to be fruitful again.

An interesting thing about this bliss is that I always feel as if it is a gift, nothing that I myself have achieved. My achievement consists in having made myself ready to receive it. Can't receive it with a headache and nausea. Impossible.

June 13, 1958

Plagued by a series of migraines. Three in the last month. Nevertheless, twice my heart has taken a great jump ahead. First when I read in Vivekananda that "Om is not a word, it is God Himself." The second was when I learned from the *Mundaka Upanishad* this little technique — "…with mind absorbed, and heart melted in love." This is actually a psychological state which can be attained, very similar to controlled relaxation or alert passivity — the same, I guess, but more personal, warmer, and with unbelievably, exquisitely blissful effect.

July 19, 1958

Sometimes I feel very close to God and I go around all day saying, "Ramakrishna, please! Ramakrishna, please!" But other times I feel very far away and I can't even say "please."

The summer has been hard — headaches, a cold in my throat, and headaches. But in between those I have felt buoyantly well and tremendously exalted. Health is essential, though, for any spiritual progress. As St. Francis of Sales says, "For God's sake stay healthy!"

A PSYCHIC EXPERIENCE

August 2, 1958

Have been reading Saradananda's *The Great Master**
with the same loving care that I gave to Narada last year
and the same deep delight. When I read that Ramakrishna
was advised to practice discrimination, I decided to try
that path, too. I began, "Not this, not this." It was as if my
mind was a stack of manuscript papers which curled off
one at a time, deeper and deeper — one page curling off
and disappearing each time I said, "Not this, not this."
And it is joy and fun. It is enormous fun.

This incident I will tell, reserving comment or
judgment. It may have been all imagination. As page
after page curled away, I felt my body light, lighter than
paper, and at one point the base of my spine, which had
been braced against the back of the couch, lifted away
from the couch without, I swear it, without any volition
or muscular effort of my own. I thought to myself that
with a little more effort I could lift my whole body off
the couch. I was filled with laughter at the thought, but
I said quickly, "Not this, certainly not this." However,
curiosity made me come once more to the same point,
then I said to myself, really sternly, "Not this, certainly
not this!" and I haven't tried it again. I never will.

I see why, too, an aspirant is advised against such
experimentation. It is very intriguing and the attention,

---

* Swami Saradananda, *Sri Ramakrishna The Great Master*
(Madras: Sri Ramakrishna Math, 1952)

which should be upon God, is brought down and held to a goal much lower. All my concentration was for the moment on my body, its lightness. Such nonsense is certainly not my goal.

August 3, 1958

My whole being these days is one pleading, urgent, burning desire, and if this desire were not to be fulfilled, then life would be absolutely pointless and diabolical. But though I weep and beg and pray and have moments of despairing exasperation, it is strange that I never really doubt; I do not feel that I will or can fail. I never imagined that there could be such an obsession. Only when I'm asleep and not dreaming, it doesn't possess me. My dreams are permeated with it. There is hardly a waking moment when it is not there at the back of my consciousness. The only question is how can I go on? How much longer can I go on?

August 5, 1958

Then when I begin to wonder how I can go on living with this obsession, something like this happens. This morning I awoke at three-thirty wrapped around and filled with such an exquisite and tender bliss that I lay motionless, breathless with astonishment. Oh, whom can I tell? Oh, who would believe? Who knows but God the amount and the depth and the quality of the joy He can bestow on those who love Him? And intensity. I have set myself to grow. Because if He has more to give, and my heart tells me so, I have to be large enough to receive it or it will destroy me.

August 6, 1958

I have hesitated a long time to write the following experiences, for several reasons, all quite obvious, I imagine. But since I have been reading Saradananda's *The Great Master*, I have found them corroborated by similar things which happened to Ramakrishna's followers and I have decided to write them down and leave them ready to tear up if I change my mind. Let me note that I bought Saradananda's book at the beginning of the summer. I have not seen Prabhavananda since I began reading. So what I have observed in him was previous to what I read, not suggested to me by the reading but rather confirmed by it.

I have always been skeptical of psychic phenomena or spiritual phenomena manifesting in the physical world. The young men of Calcutta were rational, skeptical and scientifically-oriented, like me. They had greater experiences, but mine carry just as much conviction for me as theirs did for them. One night when Swami Prabhavananda was lecturing on the *Bhagavad Gita*, his robe had slipped back on his shoulders, and suddenly I saw that his whole body was glowing with light. It came from inside and it was all through him, as an iron bar glows with fire. I was absolutely stunned, and almost overwhelmed with bliss. The same thing happened once again on another evening. Later I told him. I asked him

if others had told him that. He said not. He made no
comment, but he laughed a little. I would give anything
to see it again, but no effort of mine can bring it about.
One night someone asked him the meaning of the light
that artists paint around the heads of holy people. He
said, "People of high spirituality have a light that glows
in and around them, and there are other people who are
sensitive to that light and can actually see it." Then he
added, smiling a little, "I have known American women
who could see that light." Everyone laughed.

This other experience may seem a little less spectacular,
but it was no less impressive and moving to me. One
Sunday morning when he was lecturing, his hands,
which are good-looking hands, took on a tremendous,
unearthly beauty for me. Without thought or will, I said
to myself, "The hands of Krishna." The vision lasted for
ten minutes or so, during which I looked away several
times and each time, when I looked back, found the
same unutterable beauty and fascination, not only in the
appearance of them but in every move they made, which
seemed incredibly graceful and charming. After a while,
they became Prabhavananda's hands again, but the
memory of them fills me even now with joy and wonder.

August 26, 1958

Last night I had an enchanting dream. I saw a little
Hindu shrine, about the size of the altar at the temple. It
was decorated with bright colors, tinsel and little bells,
and, amusingly, with cinnamon candy drops. They

outlined the whole thing. There was a fine white veil across the front of the shrine that was bordered with cinnamon drops. When I lifted the veil to look inside, I was simply delighted to see the Holy Family, Joseph and Mary and the Child in the manger, and the animals. I woke up smiling with pleasure and I smiled all day thinking about it. It was so charming.

August 27, 1958

This has been a summer of tremendous spiritual struggle and this morning I came to the point where I felt compelled to say, "It is up to You, God. I have done all I can. The next move is Yours." It is very strange to feel that no one can help me, no one but God. Not even I can help myself. No one but God.

October 2, 1958

He is so good to me. Yes, I have worked hard, but the rewards are out of proportion. Last night I spent the whole night in ecstasy. I would sleep a little, a half hour or so, and wake rigid with ecstasy, then another half hour or so and this time I would wake relaxed and suffused with bliss, then I would drop off to sleep again, lying, as it were, in His hand. And now today I am in bliss and maybe it will go on all day, and maybe all night tonight, and maybe all day tomorrow, and tomorrow night, and maybe forever, forever!

And it is increasingly difficult to work. It is like walking up and down the hospital corridor with birth pains. There comes a moment when you can walk no longer. You have to lie down and give yourself up to the birth process.

October 21, 1958

Tuesday and Wednesday last week at Santa Barbara. Twice I was alone in the temple with Ramakrishna, really alone with the Alone. Love for God runs so deep, so deep. Ramakrishna on the altar, Ramakrishna in my heart, Ramakrishna in the midst of the sea of bliss and light in my forehead. Eventually, Ramakrishna the Formless, infinite Existence-Knowledge-Bliss. I feel almost sure of it, almost as if He had promised me.

November 1, 1958

Sometimes His presence comes with such a quiet and tender sweetness that I find myself weeping with gratitude. Tears of gratitude are such happy tears. And then to shed tears of gratitude in a moment of sober reflection — that is an even happier thing.

November 2, 1958

Nervous as usual. As I sit in the temple waiting for him, my mouth goes completely dry. I had baked some cookies and brought them in a tin box.

He: Well, and how are you?

I: Fine, thank you. And you?

He: Fine.

I: I made some cookies for you and your family.

He: (nodding approval) Good. (I put the box on the desk.) And how have things been going with you?

I: Things have been going quite well, thanks to you. But I need a little advice.

He: Yes.

I: First of all—what do you mean by Vedanta? For instance when Swami Turiyananda said that in his youth he was an extreme Vedantist, what did he mean?

He: That refers to the philosophy of nondualism— God is everything; all this is an illusion.

I: Then a bhakta cannot be a Vedantist?

He: Well, you see, we take Vedanta in a broader sense, that all paths lead to that non-dualistic God. For Ramakrishna Vedantists, Vedanta includes everything.

I: Now, when Sri Ramakrishna said to Narendra, "He who was Rama and Krishna—"

He: (smiling) Yes, yes—

I: "—is now Ramakrishna. But not in your Vedantic sense," what did He mean?

He: Yes. Well, you see, according to the non-dualistic philosophy, I am God and you are God and everyone is God. He wanted to make it plain that God had come down and taken a human form, God Himself.

I: Swami, I get a little confused by this talk of higher and lower samadhi—

He: There are different stages of samadhi. In the highest samadhi, the ego consciousness disappears altogether. In the lower stages, the ego remains in differing degrees.

I: But in any samadhi the external world disappears, doesn't it?

He: Yes.

(I was smiling now, not a bit nervous.)

I: I would like to ask you a technical question. In my meditation I have arrived at that sea of light and bliss in the center of the forehead.

He: That is very good.

I: But as yet, I am on the outside, on the shore as it were, on the edge...

He: (thoughtfully) Yes...it is true that at a certain stage you get that impression of separateness.

I: Now sometimes I have thought that by a tremendous effort I could force my consciousness over —

He: (interrupting) No. No. There should be no effort. You must wait. This is where grace comes in, you see. (smiling)

I: Samadhi cannot be forced?

He: Samadhi cannot be forced. At this point you must wait for God to act.

I: When I first started to meditate, I used to say to myself, "Maybe I will reach samadhi in this very life."

He: Yes, that is the right attitude to take.

I: But now I don't say that. Now I say, "Maybe tonight. Maybe tomorrow morning." Do you think I am fooling myself?

He: No. That's what you should do. The right attitude is to expect it momentarily and at the same time have the patience and faith to wait for it.

(If any one piece of advice is to be responsible for my liberation, this will be it. It has removed all urgency, all tension, all doubt from my periods of meditation. To wait in patience and faith and simple expectation, is to experience the most exquisite bliss of Pascal's *soumission totale*.)

I: You know, little by little you have been teaching me how to live. It is a small miracle. Maybe a large miracle. Now I wonder if you would tell me how to die.

He: (smiling) I don't have to tell you that.

I: (surprised) Why?

He: When the time comes, you will know what to do.

I: Many people don't.

He: That is true. But you have been practicing meditation for years. When the time comes, you will do the right thing.

I then told him that we were planning to move to Santa Barbara and that our house, when we found one, would be at the disposal of the Vedanta Society. He said that he had heard that we were planning to move. I was pleased that he had. But what made it a red-letter day for me was, that at one point in the interview, I forget just where, he called me by name the first time. Involuntarily I jumped and looked up in surprise, but he did not look at me and went on quite casually as though he had always done it. Until now he has always been so remote that I didn't know whether or not he knew my name.

November 12, 1958

And perhaps now that he has made me think about it

for myself, I do know the answer to that last question —
the way to approach death — at the very moment — to
reach out for God — to hold out your hand and say, "I
am Yours. I am You."

December 3, 1958

Last night He woke me at eleven-thirty with such a
tremendous current of bliss flowing upwards in me that I
thought surely I would be lost in samadhi. And though I
had a slight feeling of regret that I might go into samadhi
lying down, my will was not my own. I was simply
caught and held by His will. I actually could not move
a muscle while that bliss held me. Even though I wanted
to get up, I had at least ten minutes of this paralysis of
ecstasy before I was freed to put on my robe and sit in
my chair to meditate, ten minutes of absolute helpless
immobility while that current surged, welled, swept,
pounded through me. Current of joy. Current of bliss.
Current of ecstasy. Current of God's love. My God.

Then I sat in the chair with a blanket around me and
I thought, "Through the blessed form of Ramakrishna
to the blissful, formless God." I said it again and again,
but my mind was so completely surrendered to that
love and joy that the words got mixed up and came out
"blissful form of God," "blessed formless Ramakrishna"
and other combinations, until finally through all this
exquisite confusion broke a clear little phrase, over and
over again, "One and the Same, One and the Same."

January 9, 1959

Last night Swami Prabhavananda on death and the way to die, the way to reach God at the moment of dying. The lecture was on chapter eight of the *Bhagavad Gita*, and he gave that lecture to me — actually — looking at me almost all the way through. (I have discovered that many people at his lectures have the feeling that he is speaking directly to them.) Maybe he felt that he had not fairly answered my question at our last interview, but he answered it fully, carefully, and with great kindness last night. There is a wonderful mystery about it all, which I am going to tell.

He explained that at the moment of dying the life force leaves the body through one of the body apertures, higher or lower, according to the kind of life a man has lived. The level of the next birth is according to the level from which the life force leaves. If you think of God at the last moment, you go to God. Then you will say, "Well, why worry? Enjoy the pleasures of the senses and think of God at the last moment." It doesn't work that way, because at the time of death, the subconscious mind takes over, and in the subconscious are all the thoughts, impressions and tendencies of all your lives. The thing with which the subconscious is most saturated, most weighted, will be the last conscious thought. Therefore, thought of God should be made a habit, so that the subconscious may be filled with Him and, at the last moment, when it takes over, that thought of God will be predominant and powerful.

But the mysterious thing for me, personally, was this — the life force leaves through the body aperture, higher or lower, but for the yogi, who has been practicing union with God, it leaves through the top of the head, and he does not return to rebirth. The mystery is this, that when he said that, I was simply grabbed by an ecstatic joy that brought tears to my eyes. What is there in that idea that called to me with such force so that I almost felt as if my life was leaving me then, through the top of my head — that I was being swept upward by a tremendous joy? What is that power? I don't expect it ever. I don't plan for it. It takes me when it wishes. I dare to hope it will take me at the last.

February 20, 1959

Last night I asked Swami Prabhavananda this question: "What do you do when you are depressed?" I wanted to trick him into some admission about his private feelings. But he does not reveal himself easily. He laughed a little, and then said,

"It is true that all along the path to liberation there are periods of depression. This is what to do about them. Life, as I have often told you, is made up of the three gunas, or energies — *tamas, rajas, and sattva.* Liberation has to come through the tranquillity and light of sattva. Now, when tamas takes hold of you with inertia and depression, don't allow it to possess you. Get up and act, do something helpful for other people, make yourself active, *rajasic.* Then when you have conquered tamas by rajas, sit down to your meditation and let the tranquillity of sattva take over. This is the way to overcome depression."

April 21, 1959

I was afraid of the transition. When we moved to our new house in Hollywood, I passed a year and a half of emptiness. Perhaps that was just coincidental, because this move to Santa Barbara has sent me higher. The temple, perhaps, does it — the whole atmosphere so much more intimate and personal — all the surroundings so beautiful. I often sit alone with God, and the other morning His name was almost audible in the temple. It washed over me in waves of bliss. It even followed me outside onto the steps. I dare not mention — I hardly can believe — the hours and hours of the day that are filled with His bliss. I cannot count the innumerable ways in which He sports with me, springs upon me, takes me by surprise, sends my heart surging upward, fills me up to my throat with joy. I live two lives, and the inner one is far more real and present.

April 30, 1959

Very difficult to work, since every opportunity for writing is also an opportunity for meditation, and every moment of solitude brings God to my mind and heart. The temple in the morning is warm and tranquil, full of peace and bliss and beauty. I do not exaggerate when I say that I come out of there drunk with ecstasy, melting in every joint, and slightly unsteady on my feet. It is almost indecent, such love.

It is bad enough to get attached to people, but I even get attached to places. I have cried for the little temple in Hollywood. Especially last Sunday. I see it all in great detail, the draperies, the candles, the little shrine, the pictures. And last Sunday it was decorated with flowers from me.

June 5, 1959

To succeed in spiritual life, the whole of living has to become one clean, purposeful thrust toward God, till at the end it must be like a sword of fire driven deep and true into the heart of God. What strength of determination that takes! What dedication!

June 8, 1959

Day by day the conviction grows stronger that God takes care of us if we let Him. I used to think that this was a childish belief, and so it is, but none the less true. For it seems that ever since I put myself in the mystic current, that is, deliberately began to make efforts to contact that current and prolong it in me, things have all moved aside to make the way clear for me. This house, for example, in its strategic, almost symbolic, location halfway between the temple and the markets, between my soul and my stomach, was being prepared for us just as we started to hunt for a house. We were perhaps the only prospects for buying it. More and more I can say, as Chaitanya does, "Do with me what Thou wilt" and feel confident that what will be done will be right. I am filled all the time with wonder and gratitude.

June 29, 1959

Two Mondays ago Swami Prabhavananda came, with two of the nuns, to see our house. He was quite pleased with it, and that evening at the temple I said to him, "I think God prepared that house for us, don't you?" He answered, "Definitely! I do!" It seems an odd thing for me to say and believe, but I do believe it. And every day deeper and deeper is the conviction that of myself I do nothing.

This is a period of waiting — waiting for Him to choose the moment. I go every morning to the temple between seven and eight. I am alone there at the last. I hope it will happen there. I will not — as a matter of fact, I cannot believe that it will not happen to me in this very life.

September 14, 1959

In a letter to Swami Prabhavananda:

"I am not your initiated disciple. I am sad about that. But on four different occasions God has revealed you to me as you are. This encourages me to think that I can ask this favor of you..."

September 15, 1959

Dear Nancy,

Your letter received this morning. I will be glad to initiate you, if that is your wish, upon my return from India. In the meantime, all good wishes to you.

Sincerely, Prabhavananda.

September 16, 1959

Dear Swami,

It is not my place to ask God to bless you, but I can't help it. It sings in my heart. God bless you and keep you well and send you back to us soon. I am and always will be your devoted disciple.

September 22, 1959

Oh Divine God, keep the current of Your bliss moving always in me, moving upward from the depths of my being, through the heart, filled and lighted by Thy Presence, into the throat, crowded with love so that it cannot speak and hardly breathe, into the center of the forehead where the inner eye becomes dazzled and fascinated and fainting away in that brilliant sea of bliss, and so, please God, to the top of the head where the thousand-petalled lotus lays back its petals in final surrender, where the last barrier of ego melts down in the incandescence of Your love, and the small soul is freed to unite and lose itself in Thee who are infinite joy! joy! joy!

September 23, 1959

When I, as a young person, looked forward to my life, I was not, like many young people, determined to bend the world to my will. Nevertheless, I felt I had a talent, a somewhat modest talent, and that I would exercise that talent and reap the pleasant fruits of it. Of this I had very little doubt. My ambitions were not large, my wants few. It has taken me all these years, and some beating of my head upon the rock, to realize, finally, that the talent is not mine, the work is not mine, the outcome is not mine, the fruits are not mine. In fact, my life is not mine.

Actually the first person I came up against who denied me — outright, categorically, with finality — something I wanted, was Prabhavananda. I could not believe it. I think I had a moment of hating him, until I realized that hate, which has no effect on the object of hate, is ridiculous. Then, because I wanted that thing (initiation) sincerely and deeply, I began painstakingly to prepare myself for it. It has taken two years and four months. It has drained me of conceit — I think. It has been a process of surrender. It has been a growth of realization that I have no power which has not been given to me. I can say truthfully that on many, many occasions, I act and leave the results to God. So when I came again to ask Prabhavananda to initiate me, my question was indefinitive and my attitude toward his answer was one of passive acceptance of whatever it might be. Quite different from the first time! However, when his note came from Hollywood, saying that he would initiate me upon his return from India, I was blown sky-high on an updraft of joy. Now I appreciate! Now I appreciate!

October 7, 1959

Night before last I sat in bed to meditate before going to sleep. I felt a strength in me that I have felt on and off in recent weeks, a feeling of power and assurance that is quite new. I spoke within me the name of God and I held my attention firmly, strongly, in that sea of light in the center of the forehead. I resisted with determined strength the terrible pull to relax the attention, holding and holding to the name of God, gazing and gazing at that dark yet luminous cloud above. And then there came a point at which something else took over, something strong and ruthless and not myself. Everything was brilliant intensity and unspeakable bliss. My head began to whirl, but instead of being whirled into this brilliance as I would have liked, I was whirled out and back to my little self and I could not get back there and I have not been back there since.

November 12, 1959

Steadfastness, persistence, stubbornness really count in spiritual practice. I have been holding on, clinging to my foothold for the past few weeks. This morning I almost didn't go to the temple. But the insistence of the Gita on steadfastness kept intruding into my thought and I took that as a sign and went. Almost immediately, that strength, which is not my own, took hold of me. I was not gazing upon that sea of light. I was, with the greatest ease, immersed in it. Light and bliss, ah my God! For an hour and a half, which seemed like five seconds. At least twice I was near the top, the very peak of my attention, and I trembled, shook all over with the intensity of awe, eagerness, expectancy.

Afterwards I spoke to God aloud, and I said, "You could not hold out such promise and not fulfill it, could You?" But it was not really a question. It was a statement of faith. For I have no doubt, I have no doubt.

December 2, 1959

No obvious progress. But still that sea of light is always immediately available, and at times the Name of God is a wave of bliss in that sea that washes over me again and again. I could sit all day immersed in that bliss. Time actually ceases to be. I don't know how I can wish, how I clan dare to wish for anything more. But I do. I am sometimes sick with the desire for That. All that joy, and yet all this yearning!

INITIATION

March 6, 1960

Last Saturday afternoon I drove to Hollywood to be initiated Sunday morning, February 28, Ramakrishna's birthday. There were about fifty at the early meditation from seven to nine. Six of us were to be initiated and remained after the service. The benches had been removed from the temple and we all sat on the floor. It is very pretty without the seats. Prema was in charge of us, and he spoke to me and told me I would be second.

The door to the shrine was closed. When it came my turn, I opened it and went in. The only light was candlelight. The altar was banked with flowers and fragrant with the smell of flowers and incense. Swami Prabhavananda was seated on a cushion to my right, and he indicated a cushion for me.

"Sit down, please, facing me."

I knelt and bowed to the floor to Ramakrishna. Then sat, cross-legged, facing him. His dark eyes looked extraordinarily brilliant in the candlelight. He said:

"Your Chosen Ideal is Ramakrishna?"

"Yes, it is. He is."

"Good. Then this is your mantra."

He gave it to me word by word, explaining each word, explaining the mantra as a whole, carefully, making sure that I understood. Then he had me repeat it, three times, with deep breaths. Then he said,

"That's it. That's the way to do it."

I was actually in tears as I repeated it, for it seemed to me unbelievable that he could have chosen so well, an idea and a succession of words that suited me so well and moved me so deeply. Maybe he himself didn't know how well he had chosen. He was inspired. Now, after a week, I feel as though it has been part of me always. And the mantra has power. I bear witness to that truth.

Then he took a little string of Indian beads from a bowl and said, "These are your beads, and this is how you use them. Over the knuckle of the second finger, and move them with your thumb, like this. There are fifty-five beads — four for the world, fifty for yourself. And this one at the top is for the Guru." He smiled and I smiled back, but I was very emotional.

I said, "May I touch you?" I wanted some physical contact.

He said, "Oh, we have forgotten your flowers. Here — I'll offer them for you."

I felt this was a privilege. He took the little tray and placed my flowers on the altar, one by one.

"This is for Ramakrishna. For Sarada Devi. For Jesus. For Swami Brahmananda. For Vivekananda." Then he held the tray out to me with one white chrysanthemum on it. "And this one you give to me." I picked it up and gave it to him, and with it my love and gratitude, and he surely knew it. He put his hand for a moment on my head. I said, "Thank you, Swami," and left.

I was filled up with tears, and Prema looked at me and nodded with understanding.

March 9, 1960

Last night at the Gita class I asked Swami Prabhavananda about prayer. My question was: if someone should ask me to pray for him, what would be my procedure?

He said, "Bless him. Place him, mentally, at the feet of the Lord. The Lord does everything. What can you do?"

"Do you think that will help any?"

"Well, it will elevate you. Certainly it will elevate you. You should pray for the world, too.

"Can my prayer do anything for the world?"

"Well, yes. I believe it does. And anyway it does good to you."

Later someone spoke about people who are satisfied with life and cannot be reached by any word about God. He said, "Well, we Vedantists do not proselytize. Who is it that preaches? Who is it that converts? We may be an instrument for His work, but it is God Who chooses, Who draws people to Him when they are ready. We can do nothing."

March 30, 1960

Let me see if I can describe it. There is a beautiful, clear, all-pervading light, tranquil yet pregnant with promise; still, yet very much alive. It has to be held by the inner eye with the utmost care and yet without tension. Little by little the muscles of the body must be relaxed, tension allowed to drop away, down and away. And yet the spine does not slump, the attention does not waver. All outside noises are ignored, cease to be distractions. Then comes the most tempting distraction — bliss, glowing and increasing with the intensity of the attention, as the glow of an ember is increased by blowing upon it. This has to be ignored. This, too, is a distraction. And here faith must be strong, faith to believe that what is to come, is far greater than the bliss of the moment. And yet it is not a matter of mere intellectual belief. There is something deep that says, "Go on, go on! Don't let yourself be side-tracked." Dear God! I must go through. Take me!

May 20, 1960

I wonder if he realizes the power that is in him and if he can use it consciously, deliberately. Wednesday I had lunch at the convent. After lunch, the girls walk to the car with Swami Prabhavananda, where he blesses each one of them before he leaves for Hollywood. I am so drawn to him always, that when he starts to walk anywhere, I find myself walking beside him. There was just room for the two of us on the path. We talked casually about I know not what, because the sense of power beside me was such that I was not conscious of what words I spoke. I could not say it was pleasurable, or not pleasurable. But certainly tangible.

And the effect — so infallibly a consequence — yesterday and today, two days of exaltation and bliss. And the periods of meditation, so deep, so high, so fruitful, ineffable. Four hours of sleep sufficed. I awoke this morning in bliss and was meditating at 4:40. I went to the temple at seven. I came home to work, and that current was still surging up in me, at times rendering me immobile, unbreathing with ecstasy. And along with it—gratitude unending. He is the finest of God's instruments, the clearest of God's channels.

June 1, 1960

Last night I asked Swami Prabhavananda about the fact that "clinging to life" is mentioned as an obstacle to spiritual progress, even though human birth is necessary and an opportunity. I had my own answer to it, but I wanted to hear his. And it turned out that his answer was so strange and technical that I could not help feeling that he was addressing it to me in the light of what I have told him about my meditations. "When you are meditating, and have gone very deep, to the point where you think you are going to be absorbed into samadhi, there often comes a moment when you are struck by a sudden fear, you don't dare to let go of your surface life, and you come back from your deep meditation to the surface again. This is what is meant by clinging to life, the surface life."

June 28, 1960

I don't know whether it's right or not to ask God for signs and manifestation. Nevertheless, I do, and almost unfailingly I get some sort of response. I have learned over the years that I will never know what form this response will take—vision or voice or dream, or just an incident in everyday, waking life—but I have learned that, though it is never what I expect, it is always recognizable as a response.

But I do not ask for these things unless my need is great. Sometimes there is a restlessness and a yearning in me that is a sickness. Then I cry to Him, and He actually gives me a bit of balm for my heart. He does. And I know it and I am calmed.

July 15, 1960

These have been days of waiting, of marking time again. Once I would have been overjoyed at the meditation periods I have now, and would have considered them rich and fruitful. Now I consider them waiting periods. Because it is not ecstasy that I want now, but more — the ultimate, the ineffable, or at least indications, promises of it. This morning there was promise. I have grown accustomed to that sea of light in my forehead. It stretches out before me without limits. But this morning, in meditation, four times that light moved in, took over my whole body, and I felt that every bit of me was light and soon would be melted away in that light. Oh, to get rid of this person I think I am and be nothing but that light! That would be the ultimate, divine bliss!

August 12, 1960

Yesterday I learned that after thirty-five years of spiritual practice, the most faithful devotee I know has not been rewarded with one such divine contact as came to me, unsought, at the first try. My husband said to her, "Well, I suppose you go there every morning and sit quietly and once in a while you get a charge, like an electric charge." She answered, "Well, not yet. Someday, I hope. But it takes patience." Within myself I was astonished and incredulous. Then I wanted to cry— out of pity and admiration too. I don't know whether I would have had that kind of patience and perseverance.

Then I had another reaction, a tremendous reaction, because I realized suddenly that the grace of God, for which I have been so ardently praying, has been mine all along. Of course, I know that, but in a theoretical way. This morning I started my meditation knowing actually. feeling it actually, and I really knew what it meant to have the mind flow toward God like an unbroken stream of oil. I felt His grace and nothing could interrupt it. I did not ask for it. I simply accepted. And it was unbelievable joy and tranquility. For the very first time I thought to myself that I would not want a vision or any manifestation to interrupt that tranquility. I wanted to stay there, unmoving, forever, in that peace.

November 9, 1960

Vivekananda says that of all the scriptures of the world, it is the Vedas alone that declare that even the study of the Vedas is secondary. The real study is that "by which we realize the unchangeable."

I do not write, I do not read scriptures; I have no questions to ask which are not already answered. My whole activity in the past three months, maybe longer, has been a stripping off, a paring down, a burning away of nonessentials—until I feel sometimes when I sit to meditate, that I am nothing but a flame—sometimes pointed and aspiring—sometimes just glowing, infinitely spread, waiting. Mostly the latter, because patience is what I am trying to learn.

I am very conscious of Swami Prabhavananda, as conscious of him as I am of God. He knows what I am doing. When, once in two weeks, he puts his hand on my head, I feel as though somehow something will open up right at that spot and let all my being flow into God. For this I was given this human birth. There is no doubt at all.

SPIRITUAL DREAMS

April 27, 1961

For the last five months I have been performing a *blitzkrieg* on my novel — no time to write anything else. I gave up cleaning the temple, I gave up going there for morning meditation. But now that I have finished, I go again in the morning. I had forgotten how beautiful it is. Now I am going to perform a *blitzkrieg* on my spiritual exercises. Though, to be sure, it has been borne in on me this last year, that I of myself do nothing, and my only business now is to achieve a complete surrender. Very difficult.

September 27, 1961

At the last evening meeting I asked, at A's request, if by praying for a person you can change the events of his life. Swami's answer was: "I would say you can, but you shouldn't. Who are you to make decisions about what is right and what is not right? We have a very limited wisdom and a very fragmentary view."

I have occasional periods, days sometimes, of living in bliss. Especially after I have spoken to Swami Prabhavananda or taken his blessing. The last time, I was complaining to him that he had not given me enough instruction. He said, "You have been initiated." "Yes." He burst forth explosively, "Well, then, what more do you want? You have been killed already!" We both burst out laughing. He struck me lightly on the shoulder and repeated, "What more do you want?" As a result of that light touch, or something, I have remained for over a week in bliss and joy.

I would like to give up everything. I would like to live in the temple. I would like to take every vow that ever was made.

October 3, 1961

I had, as usual, made a plan of what I was going to say to him, and as usual, this artifice began to crumble as the time of my appointment drew near. I sat in the shrine room waiting and I could hear the voice of the person before me going on and on, and suddenly I had to laugh, and I said to Padma, one of the nuns, who was cleaning the altar, "Swami hasn't said a word." And I thought to myself that I wasn't going to go on and on like that, and there went the rest of my beautiful structure. So when he called me finally, I had nothing but my absurd question.

He was in the highest of spirits, full of laughter, which was catching.

I: You know, when I come to see you with a question, the question is usually so important to me that the appointment becomes a sort of crisis.

(He laughed.)

I: About that letter of mine—I must have expressed myself poorly. I certainly didn't mean that I hadn't received any instruction on meditation—after a year of consultations.

He: Well, I was wondering.

(We both laughed.)

I: It was because of something Swami Vandanananda said in his lecture on "Guru and Disciple" and I began to wonder if I was neglecting some duty of a disciple.

He: What did he say?

I: I don't remember.

He: Well, then—

I: (finished with the preliminaries) What I want to ask you is this—will you give me samadhi?

(He started to laugh again.)

I: Swami, you're not supposed to laugh. This is a serious question.

(He laughed harder.)

I: Swami, the second interview I had with you, I got off on the wrong foot. I said something that displeased you and you were severe and remote through the whole interview, and I was terrified. And when I asked to be initiated, you turned me down, dismissed me.

He: I did? What did I say?

I: That at a certain point in spiritual life, the mind has to take over, that my mind was my best guru. And I said, "But—" and you said, "No, what I teach here is meditation. There would be no point in going back to the beginning with me." I was bitterly disappointed, and—

He: But you became my disciple. You are my disciple.

I: Yes, but the point I am trying to make is this— that in spite of my disappointment, in spite of the fact that I was terribly afraid that you would never grant me another interview, I lived for over a month after that in unbroken bliss — day and night without any effort on my part at all. And now, after this interview, I will have a week or two of the same bliss. And when I have taken your blessing, I feel your hand on my head for a couple of days afterward.

He: (seriously) God's hand. You feel God's hand.

I: But you are a perfect instrument. So I thought that through the channel of your grace, I might get samadhi sooner.

He: Why do you want samadhi? Love God, serve Him.

I: Do you know where I am, on the path to —

He: Well, you are my disciple.

I: Every time I sit to meditate, I say to myself that I will not get up until I have achieved samadhi. Then, of course, I do get up.

He: (laughing) No, no, you mustn't do that. Let God decide. He will work in His own time.

I: Please won't you?

He: Suppose you got samadhi — what would happen to your poor husband? And your mother?

I: I don't expect to be helpless after samadhi.

He: (sober now) No, no. Don't ask for samadhi. Ask for pure knowledge, pure love. You are my disciple. Isn't that enough for you?

I: No, it's not enough.

He: (laughing) I remember what my Master used to say to me: "Don't be so impatient!"

I: Were you impatient?

He: He used to scold me. "Oh! You are such an

impatient boy!" No, God will work in His own way. And then, there is a tremendous joy in this thing, you know.

I: Yes, tremendous joy, but also a tremendous feeling of — of —

He: Separation.

I: Yes!

He: Well — be patient.

(I wish I could say that the interview ended right there, but I had to go on with my silly talk, and I'm afraid I left him not too pleased with me.)

I: There are some things that happened to me in Hollywood that I've been wanting to tell you about.

He: Things that happened to you?

I: Maybe you would call them spiritual experiences. One night when you were teaching the Gita class, your chuddar had slipped back on your shoulders and suddenly I noticed that your whole body was glowing. I was astonished. I went home and tried to argue myself out of it, and I might have succeeded, except that about three weeks later, it happened again.

(He was very serious, not looking at me, almost disapproving.)

I: (feeling clumsy but persisting) Then one Sunday morning, when you were talking, using your hands as you do, suddenly they took on an unearthly beauty, white and slim and graceful. I said to myself involuntarily, "The hands of Sri Krishna." And every move those hands made was exquisite. Swami, you know my background — puritanical — do you think I imagined these things?

He: (polite and aloof) No, you didn't imagine them. It is God's way of showing you His grace.

(I forget how the interview ended, but I was very sorry to have changed his mood.)

June 27, 1962

Last night was the last evening class of the year. As usual, the idea depressed me and, besides, I had been feeling discouraged about my meditation which seemed to be getting nowhere. So I went early to the temple, about an hour early, and sat in the shrine and begged with tears in my eyes, begged Ramakrishna for help. I have never cried to Him for specified help without being answered. I try not to abuse the privilege.

Then, afterwards, during the question period, Swami began to talk as though he, too, had heard my begging. He looked right at me, and he said, as near as I can remember, "You must not get discouraged if you seem not to be making progress. Every time you say the Name of God with earnest intention, you have taken a great stride toward Him. You yourself cannot tell how great. Only God knows the progress you are making. There are two things absolutely necessary in spiritual life—patience and perseverance. Be patient, persevere, meditate, meditate, and at some moment, when you least expect it, He will take you completely. Then no more doubts. No more discouragement. No more fear."

And this is an interesting thing—when I came out of the temple, my heart full of joy, my feet walking on air,

I said to Lois, "Wasn't that wonderful? He was looking right at me." She said in genuine surprise, "Oh did you think so? I thought he was looking at me."

January 18, 1963

Went this morning to visit Swami Prabhavananda who has been sick. I found him in his room — tired, depressed. He said, "I prayed to God to make me sick so that I wouldn't have to lecture any more."

I: (laughing) You don't have to ask to be sick. He will relieve you of your duties without making you sick.

He: The last Sunday I was in Hollywood, I was so tired and so bored, I just didn't see how I could give that lecture. So bored with all those words I've been saying over and over for so many years.

I: But Swami, the words don't count. We don't come to hear your words. I've often thought that if you just stood up in front of us, that would be enough.

He: Yes, I know.

I: Well, maybe you should retire — retire and receive adulation and worship.

He: (with more of his usual energy) No, no, no! Not me! I have done nothing, nothing.

I: But we feel — well, as you felt about your Master.

He: No, no, no! You don't understand. Those others — they were god-men. We are just mortals. I have done nothing myself. Let me tell you a story. When I was being sent to the United States — I was a very young man — I said to Swami Premananda, "What am I going to be able to do there?" And he said firmly, "That's none of your business. That's our business." You see? I have done nothing.

I: Yes. But we love you as an instrument of God. Retire and let us love you then.

He: I can't retire! I can't! What would I do? Where would I go? If I go to India, I will be sick immediately.

I: Do you think they are going to throw you out of here? If so, we have an extra room.

He: (bursting into laughter) No, no. They won't throw me out. But if I don't appear, things will fall apart.

I: If you get another swami from India, then you won't have to speak so often. Things will be a little easier.

He: Yes, they are trying to get me one. But it has to be a very special man. If they send me the wrong one, it will be a calamity. They are looking. And I told Prabha to write them—she sent the letter this morning— and tell them that I'm praying to be sick. Then maybe they will hurry.

I: (changing the subject) Swami, what do you think about dreams?

He: Well, there are dreams and dreams. If you dream about Ramakrishna or Holy Mother, that is a visitation. This sort of dream comes in the early hours of the morning—three or four o'clock—and you remember it when you awake. The other dreams you forget, or they are foggy. This dream is vivid.

I: I had a dream about three months ago, which I've been dying to tell you. Would you like to hear it?

He: I would.

I: We were walking down a dusty road toward a big, old-fashioned house, you and I. Across the front of this house was a long, wooden veranda with wooden railings. At one end of this was a group of young men with shaven heads and yellow robes, in earnest conversation. One of them had his foot up on the railing (so clear were the details). At the other end was a row of rocking chairs, old-fashioned wicker rocking chairs, and in one of these chairs sat Swami Brahmananda. He was big, dressed in white, and very imposing. I felt timid about approaching him. Then you gave me a little poke in the back and said, "Go ahead. Don't be afraid." And to him you said, "Maharaj, this is my disciple." He didn't speak, but he motioned me to sit beside him. I sat down in one of the chairs and put my hands on the arms. They were not wooden arms. They were wicker, and I can feel the wicker under my fingers now. Then Swami Brahmananda reached over and took my right arm and weighed the forearm in his hand. And I awoke, absolutely suffused with joy, and peace indescribable.

He: Yes, that was a visitation.

I: I thought maybe, because I had read so much and because I have such a good imagination—

He: No, no. That was a true visitation.

I: I'm beginning to think so, because now, three months later, every detail is as clear as if I had dreamed it last night.

He: Yes. And you know, you can go into samadhi in

your sleep. And when you do, you feel yourself sitting instead of lying.

I: My Guru told me not to ask for samadhi, so now I just say, "Make me pure enough for You-know-what."

He: (laughing) No, don't do that. Ask for devotion, more devotion. Why should you ask for purity? He will make you pure in an instant. Ask for more and more devotion.

(He grew thoughtful. Suddenly he said, "Yes, you have had a wonderful dream." I was very glad that I had told him.)

(We spoke about the pictures of Brahmananda he had in his room. I pointed to one.)

I: That's the most famous one.

He: I am responsible for that picture. You see, they wanted to get a picture of Maharaj and one of the young swamis who had a camera was trying to pose him — this way and that way — and Maharaj was getting impatient. He turned to me and said, "How shall I pose?" He was sitting with his legs hanging down, so I just took his feet and made him fold them under him. He went into meditation, and we took the picture. It was the last one he had taken.

(Then he was tired and asked for Prabha to get him his medicine. I left and have been fighting tears all day. For so many years he has carried all our burdens. It makes me feel devastated and guilty to see him worn out. And where will I go for strength?)

March 20, 1963

Last night at class I asked: "If God is indifferent to our sufferings and problems, how can we pray for help? How should we pray?

He: Yes, you have a point there. (Pause)

I: Are you going to answer? (Laughter)

He: You see, you suffer according to the Law of Karma. If you put your finger in the fire, it will burn. Is that the fault of the fire? You think you are independent of God. As long as you have the sense I am the doer, you enjoy or suffer according to your deeds, and God just keeps watch, waiting for you. But when you take one step toward Him, He takes thousands toward you. As soon as you say "Not I, but Thou," He takes interest in you, and takes away your suffering. When you think of yourself as the doer, He says "All right, child, do." From that standpoint He is indifferent. But He is not unaware. It is said that He even listens to the footsteps of an ant. So there is great efficacy in prayer, yes! He can wipe out your karma. But you have to come to Him. Prayer is important. And prayer is answered.

Prasanna asked: Do you think that each of us is born in just the right place for his spiritual progress?

He: The point is this—it doesn't matter where you are placed in life. Learn to be contented with your outward condition, but not with your spiritual growth. Contentment outwardly, divine discontent within.

March 11, 1964

Life has given me everything I ever wanted—love, a

son, a little success, a little piece of property. It gave me
the unexpected, too — experience of God. And now, God
willing, a peaceful death in His grace.

April 28, 1964

My husband died last Tuesday morning, April 21st, of
a sudden heart attack. My first thought, when I saw him
there on the bathroom floor and knew without a doubt
that he had gone, was — "This is the way he wanted to go.
This is what he prayed for." Then my religion was put to
its test, and it was a tower of strength inside of me. After
the undertaker came, the doctor wanted to wait with me
until Lincoln arrived, but I sent him away. I wanted to see
if I could meditate. And I could! It was still there within,
that blessed, comforting bliss, ready to take over when
I called it up. My only desire now is to call it up at the
moment of my own death. It will take a bit of practicing
from now on. As I told Swami, "I am now a nun." And
he answered very seriously, "Yes, you are."

December 12, 1964

Early yesterday morning I dreamed of Ramakrishna.
I dreamt I went into the temple to get an attachment
for my vacuum cleaner that had been left there. It was
clear of chairs and there had been a worship. There were
flowers everywhere, in the shrine, even all over the floor.
Swami Prabhavananda was reclining in front of the altar,
leaning on one elbow. He looked at me and I thought
he was trying to tell me something. Then he got up and

went out. I turned and Ramakrishna was sitting in the corner where the clock is. He got up immediately and began to talk about many things, not spiritual. Among other things, he said, "Bimila's mother is coming to visit." I was quite surprised and asked, "For how long?"

He said, "I don't know."

Then he said, "Sit down here." We both sat in front of the altar and he began to perform a worship, very strange, that I had not seen. He took two beautiful hibiscus flowers, white shading to pink edges, dipped them in water and shook the water off. Then he said to me, "Lie down." I did, and he put one flower on my chest. I was thinking that this could go on for hours and that there was someone waiting for me outside. But I didn't want to offend him and I didn't know how to address him. Then I remembered and said, "Holy sir, there is someone waiting for me. I don't have time for this *Chandi* worship." I haven't the slightest idea what I meant. (Chandi is a scripture of devotion to the Divine Mother.) He was not at all disturbed and said, "All right, another time." He took my hands and helped me to my feet, but I could not stand because I was reeling with ecstasy. Then he put one arm around my waist and began walking me up and down in the temple the way one walks a drunkard to sober him up. He said, "Are you pretending or are you really drunk?" I said, "I am really drunk." He said, "So am I," and we both burst out laughing. Then he let me go. Two nuns, Mangala and Prabha, were outside and looked at me strangely. I said, "He wanted to perform the Chandi worship." Prabha said, "Why didn't you let him?" I said, "I don't know." And when I woke up, I actually cried because I had not let him do as he pleased, and I wondered if I would ever have another chance. I wrote the whole thing to Swami and then was terribly sorry I did, because he may think it a crackpot letter. Too late now. But that dream is with me still. My meditations of late have been fruitless, depressing, desperate. I have even scolded God a little for leading me on and letting me down. That dream, authentic or not, changed all that.

THE WORLD IS TOO MUCH WITH US

February 8, 1965

Truly I see now that all is God, and all these thoughts and objects are simply the moving and changing of God's power—clouds forming and reforming, galaxies bursting and regrouping. And we and nature and the things we have built—all the same stuff in different patterns, yet, too, always, underneath, fundamentally the same pattern. He is unmoving and swifter than the swift because He is instantaneously and infinitely present everywhere.

February 15, 1965

Last night Swami Prabhavananda explained again how ignorance can exist from beginningless time and yet come to an end. It seemed to me that that would be like the infinite stick with one end in view. He said no, because ignorance is negative, a lack. For example, the nonexistence of this typewriter is from a beginningless time up to the moment it came into being. Now it exists, but it can and will end. Wherever you find something beginningless and endless, that is God.

June 30, 1965

After weeks of no meditation, I finally decided I ought to talk to Swami. But I perhaps would not have made an appointment if he had not stopped me at the door of the temple to ask me with the greatest kindness why

I appeared so sad. Then I told him I'd better see him. I was invited to lunch at the convent, so I met him in the living room before lunch.

I: Well, Swami, if you hadn't looked at me so kindly, I wouldn't be here.

He: Why not?

I: Well—everyone comes to you with troubles.

He: (pounding on the arm of his chair) Oh my goodness, my goodness, what am I here for?

I: I know, but I heard you say once that nothing tires you like interviews.

He: Oh my goodness, my goodness, what would my life be without interviews? That is the whole purpose of my life! Now let me tell you this—I can't stand seeing people sad. It makes me feel terrible. I just can't stand it. First of all, did I say something to offend or hurt you?

I: Oh, no, Swami. Nothing like that.

He: Sometimes I say very sharp things.

I: No, no! You couldn't. It's too late. You can't offend me any more. Impossible!

He: Good. Then what is your trouble? Why are you sad?

I: Well, let me go back to the first interview I had with you. I had been meditating then for nine years, and I had just been through a year and a half of—what do you want to call it?—no meditation, no contacts, no bliss, and—

He: (interrupting, smiling) Yes, yes, I know. When I read your letter, I just laughed. I said, "Oh, she's going through a dry period."

(This referred to a letter I had written, which he read aloud in class, without the signature, of course.)

I: (sternly) I put my heart on that paper and you said it was poetic.

He: Tee-hee-hee!

I: I think you said it was very poetic.

He: Tee-hee-hee! So it was.

I: The fact is, I don't care whether I get up in the morning.

He: Well, stay in bed. Sleep. It's good for you.

I: All day?

He: I'll tell you what to do — when you wake up in the morning feeling depressed, think of me sitting over here laughing at you.

(This turned out to be good psychology.)

He: Now, let me tell you this — every spiritual aspirant, no matter how far advanced, has dry periods. But it will pass. Chant the name of the Lord and be patient.

I: I know. But the last time it was a year and a half, and I couldn't face a year and a half.

He: No, no, no! Nothing like a year and a half. This will be much quicker. Any one of these mornings it will all come flooding back.

I: Can you guarantee God?

He: No. No guarantee. But I have experience in these matters. How is your financial condition?

I: Oh fine. I get along very well on the rent from my little house, and my son pays the big bills.

He: Good. Now let me ask you this — how much japam do you do?

I: I don't do any.

He: What! But that's very wrong!

I: It interferes with my meditation.

He: No, no, no! Japam is very important, perhaps the most important thing. I was going to tell you to do five thousand a day, but since you haven't any practice, you'd better start with a thousand, and by the time I come back in the fall, I expect you to be doing three thousand.

I: All right.

He: Everyone knows I am very firm about japam. You are to be doing three thousand by the time I come back.

I: I will. I promise. And you'll see me in the fall!

He: All smiles.

I: Yes. And, Swami, there's one more thing I have on my mind. What could I say—or shouldn't I say anything—to a very old disciple of yours who told me she sometimes has problems she'd like to discuss with you, but she doesn't dare make an appointment?

He: (sitting back and beaming expansively) Oh, tell her Swami is just like a little boy! Come, make an appointment. Tell her I'm very easy to talk to.

I: No, Swami, that isn't exactly true.

He: What?

I: You have a perfectly awful way of stripping off pretension and leaving a person completely naked. I remember I used to come to you with all my speeches prepared and when I was sitting across the desk from you, I would begin to drop off adjectives and tone down superlatives.

He: (smiling) Who is it?

I: Well, Swami, it wasn't exactly said to me in confidence, but it certainly wasn't meant to be repeated.

He: Tell me.

I: Bimila.

He: Who?

I: (plainly) Bimila. Lois.

(He was so shocked that he drew himself up, took a tremendous breath, and his eyes were intense with shock and remorse.)

He: Bimila! My God! Why didn't you tell me?

I: I didn't know.

He: My God!

I: (turning the knife in the wound, but really unintentionally, thoughtlessly) You can't imagine how much you mean to that little woman.

He: (closing his eyes as if in pain) Yes-s! Yes-s!

She came in just after that, and he was so lacking in subtlety that he said immediately, pointing at her, "I want to talk to you. You make an appointment."

She told me afterwards, with characteristic selfdeprecation, "I said to myself, 'What have I done?'"

Then, when we went in to lunch, he said preemptively, "Bimila, sit here!" and sat her on his right.

Later, at the table, we were all discussing the stock market—how it was fluctuating, up and down. I said, "Just like spiritual life." And Swami said, "Yes, but with this difference. When the market goes down, you lose what you have gained. In spiritual life, you never lose.

You may have downs, but you always come back to the level you have gained and go on from there."

August 7, 1965

I was invited to lunch at the convent. Many visiting swamis are here to celebrate the final vows of Padma, who is now Shuddhaprana. When Swami came in, I was so glad to see him, so grateful and eager to take the dust of his feet. Almost immediately he said, "And how are you?"

I: Fine, thank you. How are you? Are you having a good vacation?

He: (insisting, calling me by name) I want to know how you are.

I: (laughing a little) Swami, I am perfectly and wonderfully fine, thanks to you.

Yes, that's what I mean. And indeed I do see God in him, God, the Guru.

January 7, 1966

On the day after Christmas, Mr. D. died. He died with OM on his lips and that fact must have set up a lot of soul-searching among a lot of Vedantists. He was so simple and earnest where lots of us are complicated and pretentious. The last week he was meditating almost constantly and his wife told him she thought he was doing too much, because he was not well. No one thought he was that sick, however. She gave him a shirt and a belt for Christmas and he said, "I'll wear them when I go."

She said, "Go? Go where?" He did not answer, but the next morning just died in the most spiritually efficient way. She said he spoke one soft OM, then took a deep breath, brought out a loud, resounding OM, and died.

June 7, 1966

Lately a little oasis in the desert. I grab on to it and I meditate often during the day. This morning I was in that light, that all-pervading, still, blissful light. It seemed to me so evident that God is everything—not that He is in and through everything, but that He is everything, that every atom of my body is He, that every atom of the universe is He, that if He were not, nothing would be. It was easy, *easy* to say, "I am He." It was so evident.

November 17, 1966

The conviction slowly grows that the fundamental stuff of the universe is consciousness. By controlling the mind it can be refined to a point of such subtlety that finally there is no content in the mind but consciousness itself, full and vibrant. Then by holding the mind to the awareness of pure consciousness, the nature of that consciousness begins to make itself felt. It is like being up before dawn in luminous darkness and seeing, or rather becoming aware of the gradual increase of light. So the nature of consciousness makes itself known as bliss, complete and final bliss, and you and the universe are one infinite ocean of that bliss.

Still I have not submerged the ego. There are still two of us—I, and That.

December 22, 1966

I feel less and less interest in this world. I feel like someone staying at a motel. Very little of me is here and it's only overnight, and I'm not interested in fixing it up, because I'll be gone in the morning and nothing of me will be left in that impersonal room. Nothing to get attached to in a motel room, nothing to miss, and no regrets on leaving.

December 29, 1966

If I were to give one piece of advice to spiritual aspirants, it would be steadiness, regularity in practice. Gerald Heard used to meditate six hours a day, "because," he said, "I don't want to lose what I have." I don't have what he has, but the little bit I have has to be held by practice. I am adept — that is, I can quiet my mind to feel the contact with God. But I am not so adept that I don't notice the adverse effect of missing one day's practice. When I am sick, I mourn over my lost practice, and that seems to have somewhat the same effect as meditation, because when I am well again, my first meditation period is one of tremendous, inexpressible joy. A return home. Relief and surrender and bliss. Ah God! my beloved! Why don't you take me?

January 5, 1967

Imagine! At 62, going on 63, still filled with bliss and ecstasy, going to meditation in the morning, eager like a young girl going to a tryst, and recalling it through the day with joy.

April 23, 1967

Lincoln writes from Berlin that his long-anticipated concert tour seems "a little silly" now. I felt very sad about that. I have always wanted him to be a mystic and to see the unimportance of all this — maya. At the same time I cannot bear even the slightest disappointment for him.

January 5, 1968

Last Monday, January 1, I had an interview with Swami. I have been, these past days, trying to decide what to put down, because I had determined to write an account of every interview he grants me. But the advice he gave me I find so simple, so inward, so ineffable, and privately powerful that I cannot write it down, nor would it sound like anything if I did. The great part of his teaching always comes out of himself, of the powerhouse of spirituality that he is, and is felt rather than heard — is felt even as a sort of delayed reaction afterwards.

He came into the temple where I and a young man were waiting, a young hippie with a beautiful face.

He: Good morning. Who was first?

I: He has been here a long time.

The boy to me: You go first.

Swami: Girls first. Come on.

I: (following him into the office) Thank you for that "girl."

He: Women are always girls, no matter how old they get.

I: Yes, it's true. As you said the other day, one doesn't feel old.

He: We have a ninety-seven-year-old woman at Hollywood who said the other day that she didn't feel old. The mind doesn't grow old.

I: But there has to be some adjustment to the old pillowcase.

He: (sitting) Now tell me about yourself.

I: I came because I want to intensify my spiritual life this year.

He: Good! Good!

I: It used to be that my whole life was a conspiracy with myself to escape into God. I planned every day to get the most time for meditation. That was when I was busy. Now that I have all the time in the world, I can hardly drive myself to sit down twice a day.

He: (nodding vigorously) Yes, yes. The more time one has, the more difficult it is to meditate.

I: So rather than renounce God altogether, I decided to try to intensify my spiritual practice, and I thought you might have some helpful suggestions.

He: (crisply) Yes! Now—one of the most important things is recollection. Try to remember God, always.

I: Yes. I try to say my mantra all day, and when I forget, I start again.

He: Did I ever talk to you about mental worship?

I: No.

(How to explain what happened then? As he began to talk—simple things, looking at me with the deepest intensity — I felt a stillness in me that I had never felt before, that is past describing. Every atom of me was still and listening, held by his words and his look. Suspended. Breath and everything. And the beauty of what he was imparting to me, not alone in words, filled me with astonishment and bliss. He kept looking at me deeply, to make sure I understood, asking me if I understood. And if I had not been so transfixed, I would have wept for joy. And now, of course, the effect of those words has been tremendous. I have lived the past days in almost constant bliss, feeling the touch of God again and again, immobilized at times with joy. The strange mystery of that power. I want it for my own. Yes, I do. I aspire to that.)

I: Now I want to tell you something rather trivial, but it bothers me.

He: Go ahead.

I: Lately people have been coming to me with their troubles. You can't imagine the things they tell me. And it gives me nervous indigestion.

He: When people tell you their troubles, just say to them, "It is because you have forgotten God. If you remember God, he will solve your problems for you."

(I laughed a little, remembering the people I might have said that to, and imagining their reaction. No doubt, they would stop coming to me with their problems.)

He: But it's good that people tell you their troubles.

I: But thousands of people confess to you and you don't get nervous indigestion.

He: Because I don't take it in, you see. I pass it right along to God.

I: There is something else I have to tell you. You know, my son was married in September. Now there is going to be a child. Swami, is there any such thing as an unattached grandmother?

He: (explosively) Be attached! Love that little thing! There is no place where God is so manifest as in a new baby. So be attached. And when you pray for it, don't pray for anything specific. Just ask that all its life it may have devotion to God.

I: (almost more to myself than to him) The books and the teachers all say that when you have had a taste of God, the vision of God is not far behind. I seem to be in a blind alley.

He: (misunderstanding my meaning) You know, visions are not important in spiritual life.

I: Oh, Swami, I'm not interested in visions! What I want is to be liberated in this very life.

He: (and though I don't believe he raised his voice, his words seemed to thunder in my ears) You *will* have liberation. You *will*!

And there was this phenomenon: He was sitting across the desk from me and he is smaller than I am. But I had the feeling that I was looking up at him. Even now, as I remember him speaking those words, I see him above me. Impossible. Could not have been. But I was looking *up* at him.

January 29, 1968

Sometimes I try for a complete surrender of my whole being to Him. Sometimes I try for that steady flow of thought, which ceases to be thought and is just a current flowing toward Him, while every nerve in my body is vibrant and bright with light. And then I am forced to realize that I am not going to be able to do it by myself. Then I weep. Actually. And I accuse God of leading me on and then failing me. "You promised!" I say, "And you don't keep your promise!" Ah, God, haven't I cried enough?

Very often when I cry, He comforts me in the most wonderful ways, with love and bliss. And I say, "Yes, yes, but that's not what I want."

February 4, 1968

At lunch today at the Math, they were discussing the latest crisis in Korea. All those things give me acute discomfort these days. I said, "Oh, I feel so alienated from this world!" Bob said, "Maybe it's the other way round." I think it was quite nice what he said. I didn't understand at the time and laughed a little. I said, "I want to be free of this world, but you know, I was talking to a good Vedantist the other day and much to my surprise I found she is not the least interested in being liberated." D. said, "How many are? I don't care one way or another." I was again surprised and I exclaimed, "But I thought everyone was interested in being liberated. Why are they meditating?" D. — "Well, to taste the sweetness of God."

I—"Yes, but once you have tasted sugar, you want to be sugar." D.—"Well, but I haven't tasted sugar." It is being borne in upon me that my experience is rare. Swami never would tell me, and he was right. Time counts in education, especially spiritual education. I might have grown self-satisfied. Now, today, I am extremely humble about it, grateful, honored, stimulated to remember Him constantly.

February 29, 1968

The character of my communion with God has changed. The sun no longer rises in one spot, flaring into the sky. This light grows from everywhere, infinitely. No longer is it the hot rapture of former ecstasy, but, as St. John of the Cross said, "it is the calm, lonely, sweet, peaceful ravisher of the spirit." I gaze into that light and let Him, and I whisper incredulously, "How sweet! How sweet! How sweet!"

May 16, 1968

Oh I would like to stay forever in the deep, dark comfort of God!

Swami Vandanananda came yesterday to hear about my trip to Europe. He was a great audience, wanting to know every detail from the time I left here to the time I got back. I asked him why he liked to travel, what he got out of it. He answered enthusiastically, "Oh people! The divine is manifest in people, you know, and I like to see all the innumerable, varying manifestations." I learned from this. I have always taken a pessimistic view of people as gropers who don't know where they are going and are using all the wrong methods. His way is better. His way is right. He also said that he thought the reason I can no longer write fiction is that my interest is all turned in a different direction these days. I have vaguely thought so, but his mention of it brought forth in me a surge of ecstasy which is rare for me in the presence of people.

October 18, 1968

For me it is not exactly the way Ramakrishna describes it—as a fish sporting happily in the sea. It is more like floating free in light, immersed in it, permeated with it, buoyed up by it. And ah! The bliss of it!

March 25, 1969

He had someone with him for a long time, and there were two of us waiting. When he saw me, he seemed a little dismayed and said, "Do you have an appointment, too?" I said yes and he told me to come in. Before we sat down, he said, "I want to tell you that I very much like the articles that you do for our magazine."

I: Do you really, Swami?

He: My God, yes.

I: It's a great thing for me. (We sat down and I said:) Are you sick and tired of me? Or can't you tell a harsh truth?

(I meant it as a joke, hopefully. But he did not laugh. He closed his eyes.)

He: You see, I am allowed to tell a harsh truth because I am a guru. I tell the ones I love what I think is for their good, whether it is harsh or not.

I: (laughing) I know that to my sorrow.

He: Yes, the guru is allowed to tell a harsh truth.

I: Swami, I want to ask you this question before we get sidetracked. Twice I tried to ask this and got off the subject and then when I got home, I was mad at myself because I hadn't had it answered.

He: (smiling) Yes. Go ahead.

I: When a person has felt the presence of God within, is established in that current of bliss, what is the procedure then? What should be the content of the meditation then?

He: The same thing, just the same thing. Just keep on meditating on God.

I: I was thinking there might be something else —

He: No, no. Anything else would take you off the track. Just keep your mind in God.

I: I would like to tell you about my meditation lately.

He: Yes. (He put his head back, closed his eyes and nodded slowly as I talked.)

I: Sometimes of late, when I have meditated a long time, my mind gets into a very deep state, a state I can only explain by saying that there seems to be a shift of consciousness. (All this seems very glib, but it came out hard and haltingly.) Sometimes when I have meditated a long time, I drop into a doze for just a second and when I come to myself, that shift has taken place.

He: (nodding) That's very good.

I: Then, at times, some enormous force, other than myself, takes over.

(He straightened up, opened his eyes with that intense look of his.)

He: (sharply) What do you mean? Describe it.

I: It's as though a powerful hand snatched me, and whirled me, out of myself, into—

He: (smiling) Like a great magnet? Pulling? (He made the gesture.)

I: (enthusiastically) Yes! A great magnet, pulling.

He: But that is very good.

I: But then, do you know what happens? The little ego comes in, with words, and says, "Now! Maybe this is it!" and everything is spoiled.

He: The ego? Oh, I see—maya takes over.

I: What I wanted to ask you is what to do to control the ego at that point?

He: (shaking his head vigorously) Nothing to do. Nothing to do. You can do nothing. You have to wait for God's grace.

I: Yes, that's the hardest thing for me to accept— that I can't do everything myself.

He: He will take care of everything at the right time. (There was a long pause, and I was smart enough not to talk.). And let me tell you this: that deep state that you get into—sometimes there will be a long 'period when it will not return, but you will never lose it. You can make lots of money and lose it. But this will stay with you always, even after you die. And there is no greater success than this.

I: Oh yes, I think there is.

He: (quickly) Don't even think of that! Just concentrate on loving God. You have to make efforts, yes, tremendous efforts, but ultimately everything depends on the grace of God. You've heard me tell about raising your sail to catch the breeze. So go on doing what you're doing and be patient.

I: It's so hard for me to learn patience.

He: Always I tell my disciples two things are needed — patience and perseverance.

I: Swami, the dearest wish of my heart is to come to you and say I have succeeded.

He: No, no, no, no, no! It is not you who do anything. It is only God. I have never known an illumined soul who said he had achieved anything. If you do come to me, you know what you will say? "God's grace has descended upon me."

I: Well, what you said Friday night about the ego getting smaller with practice — that doesn't seem to work with me, does it? Mine seems to be getting bigger.

He: Oh, what is the big ego? The one that says, "I'm better than you."

I: And I must say you have a way of putting things, of going right to the heart of the matter so surely.

He: (seriously) It is not I, you see. It is my guru. I do everything by the grace of my guru.

I: And we, too, by the grace of our guru?

He: Well, I place you all at his feet.

(That brought the tears to my eyes. It is just part of

him to react that way, and I can't even remember God's grace! I got up to go. Then I told him that I was going to Europe.) Yes, I heard about that. I hope you have a good time.

I: Oh, I'm the most reluctant traveler.

He: Why?

I: Because it's going to interrupt everything. And I am so contented here.

He: It will do you good to have a change.

May 27, 1969

It has to be at the same moment the utmost in concentration and the utmost in surrender. How can that be? Yet it has to be.

EVERYTHING IS CONSCIOUSNESS

August 12, 1969

It seems to me plainer and surer every day that everything is consciousness and all that we see simply changing manifestations of that consciousness. Consciousness is constant. All its manifestations are temporary and changing. So how foolish to place trust or hope in any of these manifestations.

This morning at five o'clock — a brilliant meteor. I was standing at the window. The whole landscape lighted up and the shadows were racing across the fields. Then I went outdoors and we were in a shower of meteors, dropping every which way. It was as though God said, "Now this one, now this one," and touching them with his finger, caused them to drop from their places.

August 14, 1969

More frequently now, my mind is drawn to that very deep state where the presence of God is explicit, incontestable. And ecstasy, which was once the goal and reward of all my endeavor, becomes increasingly unimportant, even at times a nuisance.

September 20, 1969

Now I am beginning to know that there are two levels of divine ecstasy. On the surface level, the body participates. There is the thrill of delight, the divine fire courses through the veins, the whole body throbs. But at the deeper level of ecstasy, the body has no part. It is soul to Soul. It is, as John of the Cross says, "the deep and soft voice of God, Who speaks to the heart in solitude; it is in profound peace and tranquility that the soul is to listen to God." That tranquility is fathomless, and the joy indescribable. Just one tranquil sea of joy.

October 15, 1969

Now all bliss and ecstasy is simply reminiscence. My meditation now is all detachment and waiting. Yet this is not at all like a "dry period." This quiet and this detachment have a character, and the character of it is all promise. I wait, completely attentive to Him.

July 1, 1970

For years I have been saying, "Do with me what Thou *wilt*," with the emphasis on the *wilt* as though resigning myself to whatever pain and unpleasantness He might choose to send me. But lately I have become so convinced that what He wills for me is just to be one with Him, that my attitude is now affirmative. The emphasis is on the *do*. "*Do* with me what Thou wilt."

July 19, 1970

God is a tremendous fact.

September 23, 1970

This is undoubtedly the hardest work of any kind I have ever done in my life. To hold the mind in that state of heightened awareness, without any tension, yearning for that ultimate union, without any tension — it calls for the most in patience and faith and stamina. Faith! Faith! Without Swami to bolster me, I could not do it. He has taught me faith and patience and the meaning of love.

"Do not even think of *that*," he said. So I just strive to hold the mind in that deep, deep state, which is incredibly deep. No bliss, no ecstasy, just stillness. Incredible!

October 23, 1970

At quarter past twelve this morning, the tassel and guru bead, for no apparent reason, dropped off my string of beads on to the floor. I am trying not to be superstitious about it, but it sent a chill through me. I told Ambika about it. She said, "It means nothing except that your beads need re-stringing." She is going to do it for me.

March 16, 1971

I have felt the pulse of life and known it to be indestructible. The important thing is to destroy the ego sense, which is destructible.

April 15, 1972

When all the guards are down, He takes over. The trouble is that the mind immediately raises another barrier.

July 5, 1972

I got up from meditation planning to write, "This is

the hardest work I have ever done." Then I was amused, in turning back a page, to find that in September, 1970, I had written, "This is undoubtedly the hardest work, of any kind, I have ever done in my life."

Since I have not talked with Swami for three years, my advice and encouragement comes from St. John of the Cross. I could not go on without him. I hope some day I can write a little book that will be of some help to others who are struggling.

The process right now is this — I try to lose myself in that vast living Presence. Ecstasy and bliss now would be a hindrance, no doubt. It would make me conscious of me. I am trying to lose me in the presence of God. Occasionally I almost do it. When it happens, it will be tremendous. I sometimes tremble, anticipating it.

The subject of grace and free will, with which I have been pestering the swamis for years, is now clear to my own satisfaction. It is as if I had a needle which I was pushing on toward a magnet. When I get it within the field of the magnet's pull, it will be zapped in, like that! The pushing is my effort, that pull is God's grace.

July 23, 1972

This noon I was in ecstasy, for the first time in three years — deep, bliss, satisfying — I drank it in and I wept, because I had thought it was over forever. Only about fifteen minutes, but that was reward enough. I weep now with joy. Strange thing.

September 13, 1972

Long meditation this morning, deeper and deeper as long as I did not make efforts of my own. To keep my mind from wandering, I clung on to the mantram and there came a moment when the mantram seemed to be the floor of all my meditation. Then it was the foundation and the substratum, the very bottom of everything. Then, wonderful thing! I was taken below that ultimate base, into a silence indescribable, a darkness ineffable. The only effort I made was to deny my own efforts, to surrender and surrender and surrender. And I was taken deeper and deeper, until I realized that God is a beginningless, bottomless spring of bliss and the only thing that can reach infinitely down into that bliss is OM. And then I realized that that very spring is within me, and I began to, shake and tremble with the joy of it.

April 16, 1973

I know that the stuff of the universe is consciousness. I have felt the nature of this consciousness as bliss. I am convinced that Brahman and Atman are the same thing, and what I am trying to do now is make that conviction an experience.

May 4, 1973

The more you concentrate on that inner light, the more gross the body becomes, the more coarse; more of an appendage and a nuisance.

August 18, 1973

It has taken a long time, but I think I am finally convinced that I do nothing in this business. As Swami has been telling me all along. I used to think that I could take the whole matter in my own hands, follow methods and instructions and carry it through to the end. Now I know better. Things go very badly when I try to meddle. When I follow St. John's advice and cultivate a disposition of "passive, loving attention, most submissive and calm," then He fills me with such quiet, exquisite bliss. Then I have to hold that passive state and, as Swami warns, "not even think about that." Even if He never bestows it, I have had such grace from God, such joy, such joy!

Thomas Merton: "True contemplation is not a psychological trick, but a theological grace. It can come to us only as a gift, and not as a result of our own clever use of spiritual techniques." (*Contemplative Prayer*)

January 25, 1974

Ecstasy is a thing of the past. For years it was an exquisite platform on which I rested with joy. In every meditation I would go there immediately and I explored every nook and cranny and face and corner of that platform and enjoyed myself immensely. Then—I did not understand how or exactly when—I was drawn to a deeper level and there was no more of that exultant joy and throbbing bliss. How to describe it? There is no platform under me now. There seems only to be infinity with OM reaching down into it. My exercise is to withdraw and withdraw from the body and outward sensation, from the gross to the finer and finer. And how fine it is! No words can express! When, during the day, I happen to remember it, my heart gives a great jump of joy.

February 26, 1974

Very strange. All personal God is gone in that immense darkness. Yet it is not empty. There is a tremendous Presence filling the infinite abyss. Filling it. There is no atom where It is not. Yet the gross body still interferes with my losing myself in that Presence.

THE CERTAINTY OF GOD

August 1, 1974

When you surrender to that absolute stillness, that all-pervasive beneficent light, that inexpressibly sweet, sweet bliss, there is no doubt, no doubt at all, in your heart or in your mind, that you are experiencing God.

August 9, 1974

There is a psychological threshold of death as well as a physical. I don't know whether the medical profession takes this into account or not—though, as matter of fact, the doctors do admit that the will to live, or the will to die, plays a great part in the recovery or non-recovery of a sick person. But I have felt that there is a psychological state that could actually cause the death of my body. When I was in the hospital recovering from the operation on my jaw, maybe a week after I came out of the intensive care unit, I decided to try to meditate as I had been doing for years. I missed it. I needed it. But when I concentrated my mind, something quite different happened. No joy, no peace—just an unpleasant sinking and sinking into an unrecognizable, uncharacterizable dark state, black and bottomless. I can't say I was frightened, but I did say, "This is not good. This is not right." And I pulled back. I had a strong feeling, and I still have a strong feeling, that I would have died if I had continued in that state—and this in spite of the fact that all my vital, physical signs were strong and the hospital, no doubt, would have been very surprised. They would have done an autopsy. Which would have shown nothing. Ha, ha!

December 5, 1974

Truman Capote — "Who the hell wants to live forever? Most of us apparently; but it's idiotic. After all, there is such a thing as life saturation; the point when everything is pure effort and total repetition." — from "Self-Portrait" in *The Dogs Bark*.

January 3, 1975

Swami still speaks quite regularly at Hollywood, but seldom gets up to Santa Barbara. We hear tapes of his lectures on alternate Sundays. I don't like to hear his voice coming from an empty pulpit. On the other hand, when he does speak, it is very painful to me to see him helped with great difficulty into his chair. His voice, however, is strong, his humor fine, and his manner just as always.

February 16, 1975

This morning at 4 a.m. I dreamt that Swami died. A group of us was sitting in a room. The news had reached us that he was dying, and the atmosphere was subdued. Then he himself came in, striding vigorously, and sat down cross-legged on the window seat. He told us to ask questions, and I had so many, one after another, that finally he laughed and pointed his finger teasingly at me. I said, "I can't help it, Swami, I have not seen you for months." At that he went into a kind of collapse and we knew he was dying. His hands and feet were restless and I took hold of his feet and began to rub them gently to quiet them. Then he was still, and at the same moment he was ashes in a small box, and I had my hands on that box. The vibrations from it were so fierce that I could hardly keep my hands there, but I persisted. Then the vibrations stopped, all was still, and I put my head down on that box and wept bitterly.

May 5, 1975

And His gifts grow ever deeper and more tender. The soul stands unbreathing, spellbound in that love.

June 30, 1975

If you don't believe in grace, you don't believe in God, because God *is* grace, and grace *is* God.

July 7, 1975

There are two sides to this contemplation. First you love Him. You love Him with your whole heart, and it is sweet. Then you pause, stop all effort, and turn it all over to Him. This is not easy, because you are eager and you are afraid nothing will result without your own effort. But when you make up your mind and surrender, Ah! Then he takes over, and the love and joy and bliss of that taking-over is incomparable, immeasurable, unbelievable. Sometimes you surrender the moment you sit down, but most of the time you feel you must make your puny efforts first. Well—and the contrast is exquisite.

July 9, 1975

What it boils down to is this—it's up to you to get hold of your mind, control it, quiet it. God does the rest. And immediately. As Eckhart says, "The being ready and the pouring in are all one act." The years of struggle are simply to control the mind. The rest is waiting—in peace and confidence—for Him to act. (But don't think this isn't struggle, too!)

January 29, 1976

From *Silent Music* by William Johnston:

The undifferentiated consciousness…is a fact of experience. No use denying it. As the human mind penetrates more deeply into reality, it becomes increasingly aware of unity. It comes to perceive that everything is one. And at the same time it knows that everything is not one. This is the great paradox of mysticism East and West. Experientially, indeed, it is no problem; the person who has delved deeply into reality knows quite simply that everything is one and yet it is not one. In the simple experience of the mystic this is a non-problem…Human perfection reaches its climax where unity and diversity are somehow simultaneously operative in the same person. Just as a person can produce alpha and beta brain waves at the same time, so he can possess a consciousness that is at the same time discriminating and non-discriminating.

Yes. Yes. To me, everything is consciousness in varying degrees of manifestation, a conception which, when experienced in meditation, makes it easy to see one and many at the same time.

I remember that Swami Prabhavananda denied that there is any paradox. He said, "When you see Him in maya, you see Him acting. When you rise above maya to the impersonal God, He does not act."

February 26, 1976

I have sometimes thought that God might be vibration so rapid as to be still. Where the extremes meet. Once I asked Swami, "Do you think God is vibration?" I received the most flat denial I ever received in my life. "No." No exclamation point. Just no, period.

April 21, 1976

Oh, to hold this deep, dark state, so full of peace and promise!

No ecstasy these days. Just a constant struggle to surrender and let Him take over. I wonder if He knows, if He sees me, if He hears my cry. But of course He does. He is the Self of my self.

April 22, 1976

There is no message that is new. The word has been there from beginningless time. The sum total of knowledge remains the same. There is no progress in this world. What we call progress is simply more of everything, more people, more goods, more information, but no more knowledge. The sum total of knowledge is constant from a beginningless time.

Science is our information bureau. But so-called scientific truths are for the most part invented truths, and the truth we invent today becomes tomorrow's lie. The only truth is an intuitive contact with the divine ground. Little scientists contradict themselves over and over. Great scientists are mystics and their greatest discoveries intuitive leaps.

May 20, 1976

This yearning for God is a sickness. Would I want to inflict it on anyone I love?

May 21, 1976

Eckhart says, "It is the will of God that we surrender our wills...Yield completely to God and then be satisfied."

Surrender is the secret. I take in God with my inward breath and try to give myself up completely, completely with my outward breath.

June 2, 1976

Saturday Swami was taken from here, Santa Barbara,

to the hospital in Los Angeles. Yesterday he called all his monastics to the hospital to give them his blessing.

July 4, 1976

Swami died in his own room in Hollywood at 12:03 this morning.

July 18, 1976

Interesting to note that Howard Fast, who for years has been practicing Zen Buddhism, and who has written fifty-four books, has come to the conclusion, he admits in a television interview, that writing books is not very important.

August 9, 1976

Have been studying again the life of Thomas Merton. Mystics, it seems, suffer greatly all their lives; more than other men. But they have joys far greater than other men.

"Up, Lord, and do; stir us up and recall us; kindle and draw us, inflame, grow sweet unto us, let us now love, let us run." —St. Augustine.

As a result of studying Merton, I began to reread Augustine. His book is more than confessions. That man really dug deep into fundamental questions, free will, the problem of evil, God in everything, and he did deep and solid thinking on those matters.

September 28, 1976

That deep, dark state today. Unbelievable.

Indescribable. I try to hold it. Impossible. It needs self-surrender, complete self-surrender. Very difficult. But the only way. The only way.

October 28, 1980

The journey is not ended yet. Perhaps it will not end even with death. So my final comment may not be final at all. But here it is: My conclusions, my deductions, even my intuitions can be argued with. But my experiences, no. I have tasted sugar and found it sweet. You may say to me, "You might be mistaken. It may be sour, it may be salty." And I will say to you, "It is sweet." I have been in the water. It is wet. The stuff of the universe is consciousness, and the nature of consciousness is bliss.

I have never been, and am not now, a recluse. During the thirty years covered by these notes, I kept house for my family, nursed my mother and father through their last illnesses, and after my husband died, ran a fair-sized business for my son. The outer, worldly life is by no means incompatible with the inner spiritual life.

SWAMI PRABHAVANANDA
1893-1976

For twenty-eight years I was privileged to sit at the feet of a great soul. For the first ten years I listened, watched, argued within my self, pondered, weighed evidence. And it was borne in upon me, little by little, inexorably and inescapably, like water dripping on stone, that here at last was somebody absolutely consistent, absolutely truthful, absolutely sure. In an age so marked by inconsistencies, untruthfulness, and insecurity, this was nothing short of a miracle. Some people would have recognized him at once. It was not that way with me.

In the early days, at his evening classes, we did not write our questions; we spoke them. He knew who asked, and he looked at the person when he answered. My first questions were not for help or information, but to try him. I was that ignorant. As the weeks went by, I asked fewer and fewer. I did more thinking. Alone, at home, at times I fought with him. But I came back and he repeated the truth, over my unvoiced objections, week after week. Absolutely consistent, absolutely truthful, absolutely sure. After a while I stopped asking questions. I was beginning to realize how little I knew, and I didn't want my ignorance exposed by my questions.

Little by little, like water dripping on stone, I learned from him what religion is, and how it should be lived.

"Know that God is the light within your heart," he said, "And the light in the heart of everyone you see."

I tried it and it worked. For the first time in my life I knew what it meant to love my neighbor as myself. My neighbor was my Self.

"Place God in your room. Greet Her when you enter. Say good-bye to Her when you leave. Then, of course, find Her again outside the door."

Childlike. It makes you laugh. It made me laugh. But I tried it. I made a habit of it. And now She walks with me through the house, down the driveway, along the sidewalks, in traffic, and in the stores. I turn to Her, She places Her hand on me. This is not child's play. It is grown-up, and deep.

The influence of a great soul is subtle, incomprehensible, and unerring. This was said by Narada, the divine messenger. Along toward the end of these first ten years, I found the courage to approach him personally, with questions which had grown too urgent and particularized to be asked in public. Then I began to feel the full import of Narada's statement. He seldom said the words I expected him to say and hardly ever the words I might have liked him to say. But afterwards, when I went home, the words he had said began to grow in my heart, subtly, incomprehensibly, unerringly. And joy grew with them.

What is the mystery? "No mystery," he insisted. What was his power? "Not my power," he said. "I am at best a channel, an instrument in His hands." How humble! And yet how exalted! The very end of humility is to be a channel for divine grace. The very pinnacle of achievement, to be an instrument of God's will. A great soul stands where these extremes meet. I am filled with gratitude to have been allowed to be at his feet.

NANCY POPE MAYORGA: A RETROSPECTIVE

It has been twelve years since my mother Nancy died at the age of seventy-nine. She was impatient on her deathbed, eager to "get on with it, get rid of this worn-out pillow case." In fact, it seems to me that she spent several decades preparing for death, with a certain disdain for the world, and a critical attitude toward those who did not live up to her high standards.

However, she was a woman of contradictions, and while she found much of this earthly life futile, she did very well at living it. At thirty-two she had published two books which made the *New York Times* Best Seller list: *We Three*, a very funny book of family reminiscences, and a novel, *The Sentence of Youth*. She devoted the next ten years to her marriage and to raising me, and resumed her fiction writing career in the fifties with a string of romantic short stories for *The Saturday Evening Post, Collier's*, and other top magazines of that era, managing to support us all after my father's retirement. At the same time she did the washing and ironing, cleaned the house, went to market, cooked, and took care of her parents in their final years.

She played the piano well, told me that she loved music more than anything else, including literature, and introduced me to concerts from the time I was nine, laying the foundation for my career as a musician. And her humor was always there, quick and lively in social situations where she charmed most everyone. These were gatherings which she seldom enjoyed wholeheartedly, but for which she extended herself graciously in entertaining others with everything from funny stories to spontaneous bursts of tap dancing.

But then there was this extraordinary inner life, an intense, very private journey, not to be shared with outsiders, and a life which would have seemed strange indeed to our friends in that era before America discovered Eastern religion and gave any credence to notions of "mysticism" or "illumination." And because my father was skeptical, and even disturbed by this private life of hers, I became her confidant at the age of eleven. With a child's unquestioning acceptance, I was fascinated by the ecstatic experiences she told me about, and assumed that any disciplined person who would sit straight and meditate could achieve the same with a little patience.

Both of my parents were philosophers. The atmosphere in the house was intellectual and restrained. Their relationship was Victorian in a sense, with my father's nineteenth-century Latin American Catholic guilt, and my mother's New England puritanism. All of the passion for God that is revealed in her diary is quite astonishing. It is understandable that my father was disturbed by this, and also by my mother's reverence for Swami Prabhavananda, a relationship which, despite the great affection she felt for him, remained respectful, though distant, over the many years.

The diary was a revelation to all who knew her. It

would never have seen the light of day had it not been for Cliff Johnson and Katharine Whitmarsh, fellow Vedantists, who urged her to allow it to be published. Cliff Johnson was like a second son to my mother, and had a very close friendship with her over the last nineteen years of her life. I was very pleased when he asked me if I would assist in making possible a second printing of this remarkable book. It is my hope that *The Hunger of the Soul* will be an inspiration to all of us during this critical time, when the birth of a new consciousness is essential if we are to face the coming century with optimism.

Lincoln Mayorga
Chatham, New York
July, 1995

BIOGRAPHICAL NOTE

Nancy Pope Mayorga was born in Boston, Massachusetts on July 19, 1904 and died in her home on September 10, 1983 in Santa Barbara, California. She was the daughter of Alma Lincoln Pope and Frank T. Pope, first and long-term managing editor of *The Hollywood Reporter*. Mayorga attended Barnard School in New York and received her B.A. from Mount Holyoke College in 1927. After her family moved to California, she became society editor of *The Hollywood News*. She contributed many articles and short stories to *The Saturday Evening Post, Colliers, Family Circle, Redbook, and Woman's Home Companion.*

In 1936 she authored two books, *The Sentence of Youth* and *We Three*, both published by Doubleday, and in 1948 *This Other Ecstasy*, an unpublished novel. In her later years she contributed many essays on Eastern and Western mystics to *Vedanta and the West* magazine. These essays, twelve in all, have been reprinted in Companions of God, InnerQuest Publishing, 2005. Her husband, Aristides Mayorga (1888-1964) was a teacher and celebrated Nicaraguan poet. She left a son, the pianist and composer Lincoln Mayorga, and two granddaughters, Teresa and Rachel.

26055077R00105

Made in the USA
Lexington, KY
16 September 2013